PRAISE FOR PARENTING DECONSTRUCTED

"Train up a child . . ." when you're deconstructing? Most parents want what's best for their children, including what helps in the realm of spirituality is. This collection of essays explores what deconstruction means for this task, and the insights and proposals are powerful!"

— **Thomas Jay Oord**, author of *Open and Relational Theology: An Introduction to Life-Changing Ideas*

"This book was a pleasure to read. Rather than taking the route of organized prescriptive advice, the variety of authors focus more on sharing their own journey in parenting while giving permission to consider new and bold ways of raising children. None of these chapters/authors exist in a vacuum, and each share their own pain in parenting through and after deconstruction from a faith system that honors and upholds binary thinking and uniformity. Plainly put, like parenting, this book is a beautiful mess. Some chapters affirming what I've already been doing, while others inspire and challenge me to continue to change and adapt."

— **Dallas Verity**, host of the *Shipwreck Over Safety* Podcast

"Anyone can tell a young person what to believe, but teaching them how to believe is the more loving and sustainable way. *Parenting Deconstructed* emphasizes the latter and, in doing so, provides a wealth of information and inspiration for parents who care about creating non-binary, non-violent, and non-scapegoating environments for themselves and their children. This is a book for any parent looking to create a healthy environment for his or her family."

— **Jonathan Foster**, author of *The Reconstructionist* and other books

"The way we care for children is often missing in our conversations about deconstruction, when it is one of the most important things to talk about. Because so much of our spiritual formation is shaped by our childhood, it is critical we fold the discourse on deconstruction into parenting. I'm thankful for the stories in this book that are doing just that."

— **Cindy Wang Brandt**, author of *Parenting Forward*, and the children's book, *You Are Revolutionary*

"At one time I was a staunch Evangelical, steeped in my very fundamentalist theology. But then one day I found myself staring at my newborn daughter as she struggled to breathe in the NICU. In that moment my perfectly constructed faith fell apart and as I look back on that time I wish that I had *Parenting Deconstructed* to keep me company during the sleepless nights that followed. This collection of thoughtful essays will be a close companion for the parent who is realizing that the rethinking of their faith necessitates a rethinking of how they will parent their children, young and old."

— **Dr. Glenn Siepert**, host of the *What If Podcast*

"I say I like to be honest, but who does really? I'm not even close to a good parent, at least that's what I tell myself. Jason mentions life as a muddled stream of legalism and love and I'll be honest, that's perfect. This book is a testament of new streams and the dams of love that are destroyed to fuel them with new water. It's scary to admit we need help, but it's necessary; this collection on parenting will help, it's helped me."

— **Seth Price**, host of the *Can I Say This At Church?* Podcast

"Parenting during or after deconstruction can feel like you're walking through a maze blindfolded, especially if your parenting style was deeply rooted in your religious beliefs. *Parenting Deconstructed* gives you multiple nuggets of wisdom and guidance as you walk this journey of unlearning and discovering healthier parenting practices. As a deconstructed mom of 3 and a Religious Trauma Recovery Coach, I highly recommend this book to all parents on a deconstruction journey. They say raising children takes a village. Let the authors of this book be a part of your village."

— **Laci Bean**, Certified Trauma Recovery Coach

"There couldn't be better timing for this book to be published. With so many parents whose faith is shifting and evolving and who do not know the steps to take now with their own children, this book offers wisdom, practical insights and much-needed hope."

— **Esther Joy Goetz**, Cohost, *Deconstructing Mamas* Podcast

PARENTING DECONSTRUCTED

Navigating Your Spiritual Evolution
Without Leaving Your Family Behind

Compiled by **Jason and Brandi Elam**

Copyright © 2022 by Jason Elam & Brandi Elam
First Edition

Cover by Rafael Polendo (polendo.net)
Illustrations by Boyko Pictures (shutterstock.com)
Interior layout by Matthew J. Distefano

Scriptures taken from the Holy Bible, New International Version®, NIV®. Copyright © 1973, 1978, 1984, 2011 by Biblica, Inc.™ Used by permission of Zondervan. All rights reserved worldwide. www.zondervan.com The "NIV" and "New International Version" are trademarks registered in the United States Patent and Trademark Office by Biblica, Inc.™

ISBN 978-1-957007-32-8
This volume is printed on acid free paper and meets ANSI Z39.48 standards.
Printed in the United States of America

 QUOIR

Published by Quoir
Oak Glen, California
www.quoir.com

For our kids

CONTENTS

CONTRIBUTOR BIOS

DERRICK DAY IS A dynamic speaker, teacher, author, and leadership coach. He is a 30-plus year veteran of Information Technology (IT) consulting and management. Derrick has also been a newspaper columnist with the *New Journal and Guide* and a former radio talk-show host with WNIS-AM in Norfolk, Virginia. He is a seven-year veteran of the United States Navy, the author of *Deconstructing Religion*, and is currently working on several other fiction and non-fiction books. Derrick's personal mission is demonstrating how Love transforms and impacts every area of life—including relationships, business, education, and government. He is married to author Angela Day and they are the proud parents of five sons.

Ben DeLong is the author of *Becoming Home* and *There's a God in My Closet*. He lives in Northern California with his wife and son. Learn more at bdelong.com.

Matthew J. Distefano is the author of multiple books, including the wildly popular *Heretic!* and *From the Blood of Abel*. He is a cohost of the *Heretic Happy Hour* podcast and is a regular columnist for *Patheos*. He holds an undergraduate degree in Education from California State University, Chico, and has been in social work for over a decade, currently working as a Professional Service Coordinator in Butte County, California. In addition to his professional life, Matthew enjoys gardening, bicycling, and European football. He is a huge Tolkien nerd who one day hopes to live in Bag End with his wife and daughter. You can find his work at allsetfree.com.

Phil Drysdale is a public speaker, podcaster, researcher, and guide specializing in the area of Deconstruction. For the last 10 years he's helped people navigate the painful journey away from their faith tradition. He does research into the Deconstruction community through *The Deconstruction Network*, runs a regular podcast about Deconstruction and provides free resources to help people on their journey.

Christopher Eaker is a father, academic librarian, and spiritual director. He offers spiritual direction in person and online through Stepping Stones Life Ministries (SteppingStonesLife.com).

Elizabeth Eaker is a mother, freelance music teacher, and singer. They live in Knoxville, Tennessee, with their 7-year-old son Luke and cats Pippen and Panther.

Brandi Elam is an avid reader turned copyeditor. Her eye for detail and nearly photographic memory have made her a highly sought-after project manager in the telecommunications industry. She and her husband left professional ministry in 2019 to live a life they don't need a vacation from with their four amazing kids on Florida's Gulf Coast.

Jason Elam is Brandi's grateful husband, a proud dad of four amazing kids, former professional wrestler, and radio broadcaster. He is also a former local church pastor of more than twenty years who has deconstructed but remains captivated by Jesus. Jason is one of three co-hosts of The Messy Spirituality Podcast and has a column on Patheos. You can find Jason online at MessySpirituality.org.

Karl Forehand is a former pastor, podcaster, and award-winning author. His books include *Apparent Faith*, *The Tea Shop*, and *Being*. He is the creator of The Desert Sanctuary podcast. He is married to his wife Laura of 33 years and has one dog named Winston. His three children are grown and are beginning to multiply.

Laura Forehand is a woman of continual mental, emotional, and spiritual growth. In her ever-evolving world, she is a proud wife of 33 years to Karl Forehand and together, they have 3 adult children and 3 amazing grandchildren. Her greatest privilege is to continually learn to love deeper through her children and grandchildren. She prides herself as an elementary teacher who utilizes the Whole Brain Teaching style of teaching and has achieved the position of Executive Board Member of Whole Brain Teachers of America. In addition to her utilization of brain research in her classroom, she also continues to educate herself in the area of trauma informed education. In her spare time, Laura is a podcaster on both The Desert Sanctuary Podcast with her husband Karl, and with Whole Brain Teaching the Podcast, which is a podcast based on the Whole Brain Teaching strategy.

Keith Giles is the best-selling author of the 7-part *Jesus Un* book series. He has appeared on CNN, USA Today, BuzzFeed, and John Fugelsang's *Tell Me Everything with John Fugelsang*. After leaving full-time ministry over a decade ago to start a house church in Southern California that gave everything away to the poor, Keith and his wife recently moved to El Paso, Texas, to embark on their next adventure.

Dr. Mark Gregory Karris is a licensed marriage and family therapist in private practice in San Diego, California, husband, father, and recording artist. He's a voracious reader, researcher and all around biophilic. Mark is the author of the best-selling books *Religious Refugees: (De)Constructing Toward Spiritual and Emotional Healing* (Quoir, 2020) and *Divine Echoes:*

Reconciling Prayer with the Uncontrolling Love of God (Quoir, 2018).

Josh Lawson lives with his family in southern Ohio, where he works in a variety of roles to support and empower the most vulnerable members of his community. His experience in Christian ministry spans the gamut from house church facilitator to small group director to lead pastor. After serving in both evangelical and progressive circles for two decades, he stepped away from formal ministry to live and work as a regular human being.

Jonathan Puddle is a contemplative, Jesus-following mystic, who helps people find God at work in their inner lives. His other books include the award-winning, *You Are Enough: Learning to Love Yourself the Way God Loves You*, and *Mornings with God: Daily Bible Devotional for Men*. Having travelled the world and lived in many nations, he writes from a culturally rich and spiritually inclusive framework. Before becoming a writer, Jonathan spent 10 years in charity leadership and he remains a visionary thinker with a strategic mind. A husband, father and foster parent, Jonathan and his family reside in Guelph, Canada where they pastor families and children at a local community church. Find his podcast and more at JonathanPuddle.com.

Desimber Rose Wattleton is an author, poet, and spoken word artist. At every opportunity she is committed to reaching souls and touching hearts through love and truth. Her approach to the Gospel is practical, realistic, and void of legalism and religious restriction. Her sole objective is to spread the Good News of God's Grace through love, truth, and radical hospitality wherever God opens the door. For more information visit Desimber-Rose.com.

Jon Turney is a part-time author and blogger. Jon is the co-host of the podcast This Is Not Church. In Jon's free time you can find him making TikTok videos about deconstruction or writing songs and playing his bass.

Jon has been married to the love of his life for 30 years and has three amazing children. Jon and his wife live in Northern California on their own slice of heaven.

PREFACE

THE IMPACT OF DECONSTRUCTION

I grew up in a home where the gold standard of parenting was, "Train up a child in the way he should go; even when he is old, he will not depart from it."[1] A Christian parent's idea of "the way he should go" can vary from person to person. However, for many parents, it looks like some form of attempting to clone our children to think just like us, and by "think" I mean "conform." If you grew up in a conventional Christian home, I'm guessing that since you're reading this book, things haven't gone quite as your parents planned.

With that said, it's easy to feel sympathy for our parents bringing us up. It sure is nice having certainty around the topic of parenting. That's one of the beauties of conventional forms of faith. There is so much certainty around how to do everything. It's nice while it lasts!

So, here you are now, having departed from the way you should have gone, reading this book while wondering, "Is there a way I should be teaching my kid?"

I have a disclaimer before we go any further. I don't know anything about raising kids. I won't even pretend I do. But I have dedicated my life to researching deconstruction and helping those who are going through it. I have helped tens of thousands of people over the last 10 years go through the process of deconstruction and, as you can imagine, a huge portion of them have kids. So, I'm going to stay in my lane in this preface and talk about what

I actually know about—deconstruction. We'll begin broadly and then look at deconstruction as it might affect children and their parents.

Deconstruction is something that is affecting more and more people every year. Deconstruction itself is a hugely understudied phenomenon that encapsulates a lot of other things. Most studies on the topic of faith and religion look at attendance and belief. But rarely do they look at the trajectory. While you can find lots of data on Christians who become atheists or church attendees ceasing to attend services, getting data on those who deconstruct is more complex. Those who deconstruct are complex people that don't fit into any one box.

This is why there are so many new categories emerging for people who deconstruct like: *dechurched, disaffiliated, nones, dones, exvangelicals*, and of course, *deconstructed*. There are more ways to label your unraveling of faith today than ever before!

In 2020, The Deconstruction Network conducted an initial study looking at people who self-identified as *deconstructing* and tried to build a profile on such people. What it found is no surprise. There were Atheists, Agnostics, Buddhists, Christians, and everyone else you could imagine. What is interesting is that 34% of them were still attending churches.[2] While people who *dechurch* might have deconstructed (they may also not have done so), people in churches also sometimes deconstruct. People who deconstruct might cease to be Christian, but plenty of people who deconstruct still consider themselves Christian. You can see how the data can be tricky to look at. It is, as a researcher, both a nightmare and a dream come true.

Off the back of that study, we found the following three markers were present in those who deconstruct. It is the best we can do to give a working definition:

Deconstruction, as used by this community (slightly different from the philosophical term coined by Derrida), will look different to every person. Not everyone deconstructs from the same place or has the same things to deconstruct. Technically speaking there are three main components to deconstruction:

1. A questioning of one's faith tradition's core values and finding it unable to satisfy the questions.

2. A subsequent need to change some of one's core beliefs.

3. A reduced certainty/fundamentalism in areas of faith/spirituality.

If those three things are in place the person is deconstructing regardless of where they started or where they are going.[3]

With that definition and disclaimer of how hard it is to look at specific data addressing deconstruction alone let's look at some data, shall we?

A study from Pew Research Center, in 2014, shows over 2700 Americans leave the church every day on average.[4] Don't forget that 34% of those who deconstruct remain in their local churches (at least for a season). So, the numbers of people deconstructing are even higher!

Another study in 2018 highlights that from 2004-2018 the population of "nones" in America rose from 14% to 23%, an increase of 54.4 million people in 14 years![5] On average, 3.88 million people a year who professed some form of religion now profess no form at all. In fact, those who identify as "none" in America now sit among (and depending on how you break things up—at the top of) the "big boys" of religion: White Evangelicals (14%), White mainline (16%), Catholics (22%), Black Protestant (7%), and Nones (23%).[6] They are rapidly becoming a significant portion of the population and they are well on their way to becoming America's majority "spirituality" at the present growth rate.

Deconstruction is not something any of us choose (despite what the average pastor will tell you!)

In their fantastic study from 2014, Packard and Hope studied over 1000 Americans who had left the church.[7] Going into it, these two Christian sociologists had many of their own assumptions, one of which was that people simply left after having a bad experience—the classic "they just left because they were hurt." Apparently, leaving a relationship in which your partner is hurting you is a bad idea to some people. What they found is that not one out of 1000 people left their church after a single bad experience.

They fought through blood, sweat, and tears to cling to their community and faith. The average person went through four churches over many years before they finally decided they were done. Repeatedly, they found those leaving churches didn't want to leave until they absolutely had no choice in the matter anymore.

Deconstruction comes out of nowhere, has the gentleness of a refrigerator being pushed off a cliff onto an unexpected victim, and most certainly does not ask you if it's welcome before it shows up. Because of this, it can be an unbearably difficult process to navigate. I've literally known a handful of people who check themselves into private facilities to help them navigate it. Thankfully, it's not quite that bad for most of us, but it's definitely not easy. Deconstruction as a parent introduces its own unique complications.

The good news is that if you are deconstructing as a parent, your kids are likely to be way ahead of you in many ways! While deconstruction is far from just a young person's game (that trope is as tired and old as some of us going through this process), it certainly is true there are more young people who want nothing to do with the church than ever before. Let's go on a bit of a side tangent on age.

Between the years of 1993-2018 (25 years) the following increases in profession of "no religion" occurred in each age bracket:[8]

- 18-34 - 22%

- 35-49 - 14%

- 50-64 - 12%

- 65+ - 7%

So yes, young people are losing faith at a faster pace, but this is a phenomenon that every generation is experiencing.

Let's climb out of that rabbit hole and look at some data on kids, shall we?

Some of the latest data on the topic suggests that 66% of those who spent at least a year in church as a teenager leave between the ages of 18-22.[9]

A 2016 study found that 79% of people who left the church between the ages of 18-29 had made the decision between the ages of 11-17.[10] Just a few decades ago, this number was as low as 38%. This means kids today in church youth groups are twice as likely to have already decided they are done with church. For many, they are done with Christianity as a whole—at least in a conventional sense.

Another study found that while teens of church attending adults attend church about as frequently, they were only half as likely to pray daily or consider religion as important to their life.[11] They were also only 66% as likely to believe in God with certainty.

All this is to say kids today are not easily sold on religion, and they aren't as engaged as they used to be, despite attendance. The average teenager today can Google "what does the Bible really say about homosexuality" and have it well-researched before the sex-starved youth pastor can even begin their homophobic talk about Adam and Steve. The average kid with a smart phone can research some of these hot topics better than the average youth pastor straight out of their denomination's Bible college ever will.

So where does this leave you as a parent?

Most of you will be in one of two places. You may have an older child that you have brought up within the church and are now wondering how to interact with them now that you have deconstructed. With this comes a lot of fear and worry. We know all too well some of the damaging effects religion had on us in our earlier years. We know the work we have had to do and the work that still lies before us to unravel it all. It's a common fear to have blaring in front of us, "I have ruined my child!" It's not a fun place to be. If you have younger children that you've yet to fully immerse into religion, you are now wondering: How does one raise kids without religion? How do you instill morality, help them have some semblance of certainty, and stave off the existential dread of what happens when we die? And on and on.

Like I said, I don't have kids and I'm not an expert, but I can point to experts-many of which you'll probably find in the pages of this book

But I do know this. For those of you who fear you've already "ruined" your children—the statistics show that it's quite likely your child will be fine as far as growing up and shedding any fundamental skin they have developed. The vast majority—even if they are passionately in the system right now—will simply grow out of it.

When we look at developmental theory, children and teenagers are naturally very fundamental—they tend to see the world in black and white.[12] While some have already left the faith of their family after seeing its flaws, others can do quite the opposite and go all in. Many of us were like this as children, and it is likely that this is the kind of person your child is as well. This can be a special type of pain to navigate. Having left that fundamental faith behind, it can be heartbreaking to watch your kids go deeper into the system with excitement and zeal. It can also drive a wedge between them and you, the heretic parent.

All I can say to you in this situation is this: How did your deconstruction occur? Did someone argue you out of it? Did someone stop you going to church? Would that have worked when you were a passionate believer? Try to remember this: You didn't simply change what you believed. In a more technical sense, you grew up. You evolved. Growing up takes time and doesn't tend to look the same every time. Anyone with more than one kid can testify that you can do the same thing with both kids and get very different results! In so many ways our kids need to walk out their own journey just as you needed to walk out yours. Of course, be your authentic self, challenge them, question them but give them freedom to make the mistakes they need to make and grow in the weird and wacky ways we all sometimes need to grow.

The nature of my work is that I work with very vulnerable people. Anyone who has lost their faith can testify it is a very scary time. They are desperate for some certainty and direction. It would be very easy to try and steer the direction of such people in a particular way. This is why one of my core values in doing what I do is not to impress my own beliefs on the vulnerable people that come to me but instead ask them questions and help them figure out what direction is best for them. That would be my number one piece of advice for you as you help your children grow up as you deconstruct. Hold their hand and walk with them on their path, but don't pick and choose the paths for them.

I'll finish on this. Anecdotally, through talking to thousands of you, I have seen that those who are deconstructing their faith become better parents. You care more, you are more inclusive, you are more loving, and you embrace positive change, psychology, data, and modern science. All these things make for a healthier home and a healthier relationship with your child. It also exposes them to a much better way to do life than fundamental forms of faith allow for.

Try not to over think it. Give yourself lots of compassion. Think how fucked up a run of it you had growing up within faith and how wonderful a human you are today doing your absolute best to do better with your kids. They're going to be fine!

But also, don't take anything I say beyond facts and figures too seriously, because like I said, I'm just a researcher and friend watching you all raise your kids. What do I know?

— **Phil Drysdale**

INTRODUCTION

By Jason Elam

The day we had been dreading had finally arrived. Our oldest child, Alex, was moving out on her own. I had always expected to be relieved to see our kids spread their wings and fly away from the nest. After all, raising healthy, well-adjusted kids who can thrive on their own is nearly every parent's goal, right? Recently though, as my faith continued to evolve, I realized we had not done a good job of representing spiritual and emotional health to our kids. As our views of God shifted, so did our parenting techniques. But for our oldest (and her two slightly younger siblings), I was afraid that our spiritual evolution happened too late.

Brandi and I were both raised in Evangelical homes steeped in end times prophetic warnings and purity culture. We were both raised with an unhealthy fear of God. The trauma of the cross was so ingrained in my psyche that I couldn't even look at a picture of Jesus on the cross without being overwhelmed by guilt and shame. As a child, I used to have recurring nightmares about a hand reaching out from under my bed and dragging me into hellfire. My evangelical upbringing told me that's what I deserved so I interpreted the dreams as a warning of things to come.

As an adult, I "answered the call" to ministry to spread the evangelical gospel because I was convinced that's what God wanted me to do. I saw God as a loving but firm taskmaster who was waiting to lower the boom on us when we stepped outside of his prescribed moral lifestyle.

Have a flat tire? You probably weren't tithing.

Sick? You must not have enough faith.

Depressed? You just need the joy of the Lord!

Lonely? You should go to church more!

Reading those ridiculous oversimplifications today makes my stomach turn, but I was a master at using the "sword of the Spirit" as my own personal bludgeoning instrument. During my shockingly loud sermons, I would rail against one sin after another for most of an hour until everyone in the church was overwhelmed by a sense of guilt that had them running to the altar to "repent" and "get right with God."

That was my life's work for years —guilt tripping people into the Kingdom of God. Of course, that kind of repentance rarely takes root, and folks didn't stick around the churches that I pastored for very long. Today, I'm grateful for that. Back then, however, it was a source of great frustration and heartbreak to me. Within just a few years, I was completely burned out.

As the stress worsened, my miserable first marriage collapsed along with my ministry. At rock bottom, I looked up and began to experience and appreciate the grace and compassion of God. I could sense that God still loved me and still had some purpose for my life, but I still struggled with legalism and a deeply embedded sin consciousness.

This muddled stream of love and legalism corrupted all my relationships. Even after marrying the love of my life, Brandi, and raising four kids together, I still found myself operating out of both compassion and guilt which led to a rather two-faced existence.

"God loves you. Now act right."

"No, you can't use that app because bad things happen on that app."

"No, you can't date. Boys only want one thing from girls."

"I don't care that you don't want to go to church today. That's what we do on Sundays!"

As you can imagine, this wasn't a fun existence for anyone involved. Brandi was further along in her spiritual evolution than I was and often pushed back against my heavy-handed rules. That caused friction between us. Unfortunately for our oldest three kids, most of their childhood was lived in that tension.

More than a decade later, I was walking around the track one day at my local gym listening to author Jonathan Martin interview his fellow author, Brad Jersak. As they spoke about the love of God, I experienced something incredible. I can only describe what happened that day as waves of liquid love crashing over me. All my guilt, shame, and fear were washed away that day. I saw—for the first time—a God who loves us all as we are. I encountered a Jesus whose table was big enough for every member of the human family with no exceptions. In the years since, I have come to know a God who has no desire to control me in any way. That's a big turnaround from believing in a God who cared whether I wore the striped socks or the plain!

I knew that my relationships with my family needed to change in light of this liberating understanding of God, but how? We had raised our kids with strict rules because that's how we thought God dealt with us. Now that we understand that God isn't like that what does it mean for how we relate to our kids?

Sitting in my recliner that day, across from our oldest with tears streaming down my face, I told her how sorry I was for not being a better parent. We told her that she always had a home with us and would never be without a place to go if she needed one. But I knew the chances of her ever coming back to live with us for more than a couple of weeks between college semesters were nearly non-existent. She is a smart, beautiful girl with an independent spirit, and we had clipped her wings long enough.

I wanted to do better by our other kids. But how?

I searched everywhere for a book on the subject. I finally came across *Parenting Forward: How to Raise Children with Justice, Mercy, and Kindness* by Cindy Wang Brandt and found it helpful, but I needed more. I kept looking for resources and coming up empty.

That's how this book came to be. We reached out to writers, teachers, and counselors that we know and trust and invited them to submit essays on parenting post-deconstruction. Our co-authors in this book come from a wide spectrum of backgrounds and beliefs, but they have at least one thing in common: They want to see you love your kids well and give them the best possible start in life. You'll notice some common themes—most of us wrestled with the idea that if we'd just "train up a child in the way they should go, and when they grow older they won't depart from it," but what does that really mean and does it even matter in 2022?[1]

I love the different perspectives and understandings represented in this book, and I hope you will too. Some of us are still actively seeking to follow Jesus. Others are not. Some of us can't even describe where we are spiritually right now—and that's ok. Every contributor brings hard-fought wisdom and fresh insights that will help you be the best parent that you can be.

This isn't a book about how to be a perfect parent. That book doesn't exist. If that's what you're looking for you should just go ahead and take this book back to wherever you bought/borrowed it.

This book represents a journey toward understanding our kids and our relationships with them better in light of our shifting spiritual beliefs.

And that's a very good place to start.

PART I: MOVING BEYOND REGRET

1

DECONSTRUCTED PARENTING: A CAUTIONARY TALE

By Keith Giles

FOR THE LAST FEW years, I have been helping people process their deconstruction and navigate their journey towards reconstruction in a series of online courses I created called *Square 1*. As a result, I've heard dozens of tearful stories about how painful it was when family members, friends, and other believers rejected them for questioning or doubting the tenets of the Christian faith they were raised with. I've listened, encouraged, sympathized, and affirmed so many people who know the deep wounds of rejection, and the waves of unrelenting guilt heaped upon them by people who were supposed to love them. I understand their overwhelming feelings of shame, and the fear of being burned for eternity by a God whose unquenchable wrath against them was ever present in the form of a mother's tone, or a father's glance, or a sibling's comment. I've worked tirelessly to bring healing to people who find themselves in this lonely place, to provide a community where they can share their stories without fear and offer comfort to the seemingly endless number of people who, like them, have experienced the brutal rejection of the Christian community that once embraced them.

So, I'm no stranger to how damaging and destructive the deconstruction process can be. I've endured a measure of this myself, but it was only a few months ago that I had the most horrific realization: *I had treated my oldest son the exact same way when he told me he didn't believe in God anymore.*

Dylan's deconstruction came at a time when my wife, Wendy, and I were about five years into our own exodus from traditional Christianity. We had left the little Vineyard church in Tustin, California, that we had helped to plant with some of our friends and stepped out into the uncharted territory of "house church" a few years earlier. Now our little home fellowship was thriving. We were discovering new ways to "be the Church" in our neighborhood and community. Our service to people living in a local motel was going better than we could have imagined with other churches coming alongside us to launch a church in the back parking lot. Everything was going great, from our perspective. But, for our son, Dylan, things were falling apart—at least on a spiritual level.

The first time we realized Dylan wasn't on the same page was one Sunday morning when we were serving at the Motel Church in Santa Ana. The four of us, Wendy, our sons Dylan and David, and myself, had just pulled into the parking space in the back lot where our little motel church gathered. People were unloading equipment, setting up tables and chairs, and getting things ready for the food distribution, which always kicked everything off. As usual, we all jumped out of the car and started to unload the trunk to set up for the day. All of us, that is, except for Dylan. He stayed in the back seat by himself. After a few minutes, I noticed he was still sitting there all alone. I walked over and opened the back door.

"Are you okay?"

Dylan looked at me with a serious face and said, "I don't want to do this."

I blinked. "What do you mean?"

He took a deep breath and looked away, through the front windshield and said, "I just don't feel like being here."

At first, I thought he might be sick. "Are you feeling okay? Do you need to lie down or something?"

He shook his head. "No. I just don't feel like being here."

At this point I felt like he was just being stubborn. "Dylan, you can't just sit here in the back seat of the car all morning. We're going to be here a few hours. Just come on out and have a seat with the rest of us."

Dylan refused. That just made me angry, and I started to put the pressure on. I used fear, guilt, shame, threats of punishment, grounding, loss of video game privileges, anything and everything I could think of to get him to move. He didn't budge. I was furious, but I decided to let him sit there and deal with him later.

After our service was over, we loaded everything back into the car, said our goodbyes and started driving back home. I was livid, and I made sure Dylan knew how disappointed, angry, and upset I was. He did his best to calm me down, but to be honest I wasn't really listening very much.

Once we got home, I sat down with Dylan alone so we could get to the bottom of things. I couldn't understand why he was suddenly being so difficult and aggravating. Eventually, he found the courage to say it out loud: "I just don't think I believe in God anymore, Dad."

That stunned me. I knew it had to be because of this new school we had started to send him to. Surely one of his teachers had put doubts in his head about the Bible, or God, or Christianity in general. We talked for about an hour. At first, I did my best to provide answers to his questions and offer rebuttals for his every doubt, but after a few minutes I realized it was doing no good. He didn't really want me to give him proof. He didn't need me to connect the dots for him. He had lost his faith. That was it. I knew it was probably better to just let it go. For now at least.

I wish I could say I handled Dylan's deconstruction better than I did. But I can't. Truth be told, I was horrible. Every awful thing I've heard others tell me their parents did, I did to Dylan. Every ounce of fear, every drop of guilt, every bit of shame, I threw at him relentlessly in a desperate attempt to win him back to the faith. I know now that what was driving me was my own fear, my own guilt, my own shame that still clung to my heart like a black oil stain on my soul after decades sitting under doctrines of eternal torment, penal substitution, and worm theology. Eventually, I would come to realize how destructive and un-Christlike these things really were, but at the time I was still convinced that my first-born son was on his way to an eternal hell for rejecting his Christian faith. I was desperate to save him, change him, fix him, before it was too late.

Now, of course, I realize that my fears were unfounded, my desperation to "save him" was foolish and my overreaction was unnecessary. But none of that really matters, does it? The truth is that I did react this way, and my fears compelled me to subject my dear son to several years of emotional torment while I slowly deconstructed those toxic beliefs. Eventually, I got it. I let go of Eternal Torment. I rejected Penal Substitution. I abandoned Worm Theology. All good for me. No help for Dylan who, in the meantime, had endured my misguided attempts to force him back into the faith by any means necessary.

Honestly, the worst part, for me, was to realize that I did all of that and never consciously admitted it to myself, or to him, until years later. Even then, this realization came to me only after spending several years listening to person after person tell me how horrible it was to suffer the rejection, guilt, and fear coming from their own parents when they deconstructed. Why did it take me so long to see this? Why couldn't I see myself in these stories? Most of the time I identified with the person being rejected. I remembered how painful it was when my pastor friends rejected me publicly, and rebuked me privately, for changing my views. I remembered clearly how much it hurt to be ignored by Christian friends in the grocery store or called a heretic by people I once believed were my friends. That was what I related to. Those were the stories where I could identify myself as the victim of such rejection but never as the one pouring out the shame, never the one hammering my son with fear or guilt. I could only see myself as the one enduring these things, never as the one who was capable of doing such things to other people.

So, why am I telling you all of this? Well, a few reasons, I guess.

First, so that you don't do the same things to your own children. And if you do, or if you have, to give you permission to grieve for those things. Maybe you need to go to your children and ask them for forgiveness? Maybe you need to admit to them, and to yourself, that you were once the kind of person who was motivated by fear rather than love, by guilt rather than freedom, by shame rather than joy. This is part of your own healing, as well. To see, once and for all, that you are capable of worse things than you ever wanted to believe possible. To forgive yourself, and to ask your children for forgiveness. To start the healing process in yourself, and hopefully, in your children too.

Second, I share my story with you in hopes that you might have mercy and grace for those who have hurt you. Maybe you didn't treat your kids this way when they deconstructed. Maybe you had already fully rejected those toxic theologies long before they caught up with your change of heart and mind. If so, that's wonderful. I'm envious. But, maybe now that you've heard my story you could find it in your heart to let your own parents and siblings and friends off the hook for the ways they reacted when you told them you had changed your mind about what you once believed. I'm not saying that what they did was okay or that it didn't hurt. Because it wasn't okay and, of course, it really did hurt. A lot. But the same toxic theology that you had to escape from is what twisted your parents and family into believing what they did—and acting the way they did—when your deconstruction started. If possible, we need to separate what they did from why they did it. As messed up as it sounds, the ones who loved you the most hurt you so badly because their ideas of God and Love and Faith were distorted by a lifetime of bad theology and reinforced by a religious system that thrives on fear. I know it doesn't change how much it hurts. But hopefully, it helps you make sense of the "why" those things happened the way they did.

Finally, I share my story because I need to. I need to put this down on paper. I need to admit to myself, and to my son, and to the world, that I failed to be the kind of Father I intended to be. Not to give myself excuses, but to own it completely. When my dear son looked me in the eye and told me what he was feeling, I didn't listen. When he trusted me enough to admit the truth, I did everything in my power to prove him wrong. When he stood up for what he believed, I did my best to make him sit down. For all of that I am deeply sorry. I wish I could go back and do it all over again today. I know that the person I am now wouldn't react the way I did then. In fact, the person I am now would pull that version of me to the side and make him back off, take a deep breath, let it go. I wish I could do that. I really do. But, of course, that's not possible.

Maybe, hopefully, my story will give you some sense of healing for the ways you've blown it with your kids. Maybe it will give you a window into the soul of your own parents when they treated you the way I treated my son. Maybe it will give you an opportunity to forgive them, or at least to understand what happened and why. I don't know. What matters most to me is making sure I never do anything like that again and telling the world— and especially my own son— just how sorry I am for reacting the way I did. I can never take it back, but maybe I can make up for it by helping others process their own pain and making sure my sons know how much I love them and adore them no matter what they believe, or don't believe. For now, that's the best I can hope for.

2

DECONSTRUCTING DISCIPLINE

By Derrick Day

Like many children growing up in the 1960s and 1970s, I was raised with strict discipline. We were taught that physical punishment was necessary in the effective rearing of children. As a hardheaded young man, I got my ass "whooped" often.

When I grew up, I adopted this same paradigm. As the father of sons, I believed that corporal punishment was the best way to instill discipline in my sons. Indeed, as a black father, I believed that it was necessary to instill a sense of "godly fear" into my sons—to help "save their lives" when they were out in the world.

But then there was deconstruction. And, before I go any further, I must offer the caveat that I no longer consider myself a Christian. This may cause many of you to fast-forward beyond this chapter. But if you're looking for a breakthrough with your children—especially if you have young children—read on. You will not be disappointed.

The first thing that I discovered was that the god I believed in didn't need my money. Comparing and contrasting my celestial parent with my natural parents, I clearly saw that my parents didn't need my money to see their "vision" come to pass. My whole understanding of tithing and giving was stood on its ear.

This was followed by the discovery that there was no eternal conscious torment. Thanks to some (at the time) kindred spirits, I began to see that if god was truly "love," then god had to be truly inclusive. Moreover, because the perception that god operates outside time, god can't be too terribly concerned with what takes place in time. After all, our lives are but a blip on the radar of eternity.

I like smoking meat; it's one of my hobbies. Part of the preparation for smoking is building a sustainable fire. Once, I was showing one of my sons the fire craft involved in smoking. Just when the coals were white-hot, I heard a voice ask me if I would put my son in this fire for disobedience. (Full disclosure - the voice I heard here I thought was god, but now I understand to have been my own inner voice).

I could not fathom a reality where I'd ever submit my child to that kind of torment. Personally, I'd take a bullet for any of my sons. If god would submit any of his children to eternal fire, that meant I was a better parent than god.

The next thing I learned that if this god was truly a parent or, for that matter, the paradigm of a good parent, then he cannot "play favorites." According to the Christian holy book, god is "no respecter of persons;" that is, what he will do for one, he must obligate himself to do likewise for all his children. The great contradiction in this was that in church, we'd often say, "favor isn't fair."

In other words, there was a way, a formula, for currying favor ahead of our siblings in faith. This god would have to not only reward some believers above others but would have to reward some believers at the expense of others. Remember the "wealth of the wicked laid up for the just?"[1]

The big thing was the "chastening of the lord." In preaching circles, I often heard "that you haven't had a whoopin' until you had a whoopin' from god." I must confess that I bristled every time I heard this. Not only that, but I also recalled all the times I had been "disobedient" to god and that I had never been "punished." Matter of fact, I can recall some specific incidents where things actually turned out better for my "rebellion." I learned that even my feeble interpretation of god couldn't be a punisher. The bible says god is a rewarder of those who diligently seek him so if I sought him while screwing up, that meant I'd be okay. The "chastening" I received was always a gentle nudge or correction; it was never harsh, condemning, or punishing.

Which brings me to the point of this chapter: Chastening isn't punishment. Like I said earlier, I spanked my kids because I thought it was the right thing to do. In fact, I thought it was the biblical or godly thing to do. Once again, study led me to learn something: that the shepherd's rod was never used to beat the sheep but to nudge the strays back into the fold. I remember a passage where the psalmist said, "Your rod and staff, they comfort me."[2] Contrast this with "spare the rod, hate the child."[3] When I connected these two passages, I learned that correction should be comforting.

There's nothing comforting about a spanking! Nothing!

In other words, if I spare comforting correction, I hate my child. Corporal punishment is not what this is about! The Jesus of the bible says his yoke is easy and his burden is light. When tied together I learned, as a parent to not put undue burdens or expectations on my children and not to punish them when they failed to meet my expectations.

Not long after we moved to Arizona, my youngest son threw a rock that broke a neighbor's window. I was angry because he caused me to incur a debt. I was angry because it challenged our reputation in the neighborhood. Yes, I spanked him but, even worse, I occasionally reminded him of what he did wrong for several years afterward. When I came to myself regarding correction, I immediately apologized to my son and promised I'd never bring the incident up again.

I learned how to talk to my sons—how to give them a nudge that was comforting. I learned how to listen to them and learn why they made the mistakes they did. I learned how to build them up in love and trust, rather than breaking them with threats and punishment.

Here's my dilemma, though: My older sons caught the brunt of "wrathful dad" while my younger sons experienced the freedom of "graceful dad." My older sons are somewhat resentful because of what they experienced in me. Even though I have beseeched their forgiveness (and continue to do so), and even though they say they understand, corporal punishment left a lasting scar on them. Even my younger children remember spankings, though they didn't endure them nearly as long as their older siblings. This is a cross I must bear.

These days, I generally refrain from identifying things as "right" or "wrong." In this case, however, let me state, emphatically, and for the record, that spanking is wrong. It is never right to hit a child. Honestly, I don't even think you should raise your voice at your child. I think if we are to use a Christlike paradigm for child rearing, it must be as gentle as the Christ it purports to represent.

People say they got spanked as a child, and they turned out okay. I used to say that and, I'm here to tell you, I'm not okay. I still suffer from the trauma of the hands that were supposed to nurture and nudge me, not restrain and spank me. I turned out okay in spite of the spankings, not because of them.

I can only say I'm happy I learned this before permanently scarring all my sons. Deconstructing from religion helped me reconstruct into a better father.

3

EVOLVING OUT OF FEAR-BASED SYSTEMS

By Karl Forehand

I WAS KNEELING DOWN over a flowerbed when I noticed my daughter standing next to me. She was poised like she wanted to talk, so I just sat back on the grass. Lily was facing me directly with her hands on her hips, and then she let me have it!

For a few years, I had been telling people that I was paddling my man boat through the estrogen sea, because I had two teenage daughters, and I had no idea what to do. Lily has been articulate since she was a toddler, and she retains information like a sponge. I would have to conclude that her whole life, I have never won an argument with her - her husband seconds that sentiment.

Shortly after she started informing me about a few things, I found myself becoming agitated. You know, it's those thoughts we have like, "Who does she think she is?" This type of incident happened another time, and I had the same initial emotion. I am glad that I didn't say something silly, such as "Just calm down, and we'll talk later." She needed to express what she was thinking, and thankfully I realized this shortly after she started talking.

I can't say that I comprehended everything she was trying to teach me, but she did teach me that day. She taught me about what makes her tick, about what she felt, and she showed me her heart. It was a deeply intimate moment where she became the teacher that I always wanted to be for her. I am glad that I was able to dodge my initial instincts and hear her emotions as well as her wisdom.

It was about this time that I started to understand some of the things that were working for us as parents. It would become clarified later, after I went through deconstruction and after our children were grown. But I imagine that during most of the years when our kids were growing up, I probably had a bewildered look on my face. We received way too much advice from many people who really didn't know what would work either.

Not only were we learning about what was working, but we were also slowly discovering what never had a chance of maturing into anything viable. Some of these ideas were rooted in bad theology. Some of our decisions were conceived in ignorance. Many of them were bad assumptions or just listening to the wrong people. The common denominator in most of our bad decisions was that we tended to begin with fear.

Our Worst Decisions were Rooted in Fear

I often state that almost every religion I have ever studied begins its theology with what we should be afraid of. It doesn't really matter what the other person is selling. If they can convince us to be afraid of hell, or dying, or not being popular, they can sell us almost anything.

It happened that way often in parenting. We would hear a news report that something was happening in *record* numbers. Other times, a pastor's message might warn us about something we hadn't ever considered, and then we became determined to *take action* or *do something* about it. When I was a preacher, I did this almost subconsciously. Influencers know that the strongest motivator, especially for parents, is fear.

But fear causes us to be reckless in our strategies. Because we are afraid of what might happen, we over-emphasize the urgency to fix a problem we didn't even know existed yesterday. I was that way with purity rings after I watched a video that first created a fear, then made me feel guilty and prompted me to act as quickly as I could. I deeply regret giving the rings—the girls never spoke of them after that day. The purity culture used our fears to market an agenda that was traumatizing to women and created more problems than solutions.

We were also often afraid of what people thought. In some ways, we realized it was happening and apologized to our children because we were in ministry, and we didn't see another way out of it. Our children were incredibly gracious, but I always felt like I was sacrificing my integrity for some jackass that probably would turn on us a little later in the journey.

Today, I talk about *being who we are* (authenticity), and I deeply understand how much better being respected is than being liked. Even though my teenage children understood compromise, they respect me so much more being real now that they are older. I wish I would have been more authentic for them and myself during their formative years. I don't even attend church now, and so I regret much of that activity that I wasted trying to get the congregation to accept me.

I probably could write a book about the ways fear motivated me to hasty and unwise decisions in my life and my years as a parent. For the most part, our children understood that we weren't perfect, but mostly because we learned to apologize when we got it wrong. Fear is never a good starting place for any decision. We are most always somewhat misinformed, and our emotions cause us to venture outside reasonable logic and into dangerous decisions.

But we did get a few things right.

Learning to be Brave

My dad never learned to swim. My grandpa is a person I am connected with spiritually in some strange metaphysical way. I can literally feel him sometimes. But I remember a time when he was teasing my dad about never learning to swim and about being lazy. It had a deep resonating impact on me. Not because it was Good Parenting 101, but because of the opposite of what I described above—I didn't want to be afraid of anything.

As I stated, I often succumbed to my fears, especially when people I admired told me I should be afraid. But, after listening to my grandpa and my father, I was determined that I never wanted to regret missing an opportunity simply because I was afraid. I made eleven skydiving jumps, I took karate, and attempted unknown territories like writing books. I had a crippling fear of speaking in public but overcame it to be an effective speaker and preacher. I traveled overseas and changed careers several times because I did not want to regret what I was afraid to experience. It would be okay if I didn't succeed, but it wouldn't be okay if I didn't try.

I was determined to instill this type of bravery in my children. I wanted them to learn confidence to answer the phone and speak in public and make their own decisions. So, when our oldest daughter, Abbey, was young, I started whispering in her ear to "be brave." Twenty years later, I saw a social media post that expressed something like, "I don't need a man to slay the dragon—I am the dragon." She has certainly been courageous to achieve the goals she set out to accomplish and she is thriving as an RN in the Kansas City area.

Occasionally, I overheard my children talking. Sometimes it was disturbing, and other times it was life giving. The latter occurred when I heard Abbey whispering to her sister to "be brave." You can't imagine how inspiring and uplifting that was! It was one of the greatest moments in my life, and now I get to witness her teaching bravery to her two daughters and her husband.

Children are sometime reckless by nature, but bravery must be modeled and taught. Amidst the sea of machoism, crowd-following, and foolish behavior can be genuine, character-building bravery. It is authentic and honest and inspiring. I challenge you to experience true bravery in your journey and to share that challenge with those who look up to you.

Finding our Voice

My parents told me stories of how I would hide under the coffee table when people came over. I played sports and participated in most activities, but I always found a way not to talk. When I went to college, I had to take speech. I was doing okay in the class, and I think it interested me because it was a new adventure. But I almost flunked the class because I left off over half of a 15-minute speech—I just forgot it!

Early in my career, a manager called me into her office and informed me of an issue she had with my performance. To make a long story short, she told me I was a good worker, but I needed to learn how to speak better, or "it just isn't going to work out." She referred me to a group that met on that campus, and I started attending reluctantly after work. It was a little club for people like me. We mostly did extemporaneous speaking which felt like torture. When it was your turn, someone would hand you a topic, and you would have to speak for a minute or two. It felt like an eternity, and I literally almost vomited a few times. The experience challenged me and caused me to get better. Later, I would join a Toastmasters group while working for another employer. I won a couple of awards and later became president of that group.[1]

I thought I had conquered my fear until I had to teach from the Bible for the first time. I was being licensed for ministry, and my pastor let me teach a lecture at our church and again, I felt like I was going to be sick. It got easier over time, until I preached my first sermon. With each new challenge came a new level of pain and adjustment and, ultimately, mastery (or as close as I could come to it).

When Laura and I started writing about "Finding our Voice," I assumed that I had found my voice already, especially since I was a pastor and got to say what I thought every Sunday. As I reflected on this after leaving the pastorate, I realized I did not really have an authentic voice because I always had to answer to the board, the deacons, or the congregation. Subconsciously, I knew that I could only go so far with challenging long-held beliefs. No matter how smart, talented, or insightful I might be, the people wanted their pastor to talk about what they expected him to talk about.

After deconstructing and leaving the pulpit, I began to understand finding my voice and reflected on how I shared that with my children. I remember a painful conversation with my son, Jordan, when I needed him to tell me about something that happened to him at college. It was like he was experiencing the kind of difficulty I experienced all those years trying to learn to communicate.

What was it that had to happen in those speeches and conversations? We had to be *vulnerable*—it's so important. I didn't know what he was going to say, and he didn't know how I would receive it. Being vulnerable is important now in my writing, my healing, and all aspects of my journey. But I also had to teach it to my children. I think it has something to do with being seen with eyes of grace. When we "spill the beans" and we don't die, it heals the shame and creates a new confidence in us. We are so vulnerable with our children since we have deconstructed, and there is so much less judgment.

Finding our voice also births in us a deeper root into *authenticity*. We can now speak to each other as ourselves without playing a role. Because we now realize how much every person needs their autonomy, we don't play roles or put expectations on them. We are learning to be *who we are*.

To be honest, figuring out *who we are* is difficult after deconstruction. So much of what we identified with before was what we did and what was expected of us. Now that a lot of that is stripped away, we ask questions like: "What do we really like to do? What do we really care about? What is our truth that needs telling?" The great thing we can now do is ask those questions honestly to our grown children and, for the first time, not have any expectations. Knowing *who we are* and finding out who our children are authentically may be one of the greatest gifts to give a member of the family.

Learning to Think for Ourselves

I always said that I wanted them to find their own faith, even when I was deep into ministry. But what I really wanted was for them to find my faith. Eventually, they were all baptized into the faith that I was participating in. What I didn't see was, at the same time, I was teaching them to think for themselves. I remember seeing an essay Jordan wrote at college about the legalization of marijuana and realized he truly was thinking for himself.

All three of our kids moved away from our home, went to college and established lives for themselves. They all have their own lives, their own beliefs, and their own political views. I am so thankful we fostered this passion in them to find out how they feel about various things in life. There were times when it worried me, but now I see it is the greatest gift we could have given them.

I remember when we told the girls that we were deconstructing. They just kind of acknowledged that they had been waiting for us to evolve. They were accepting and gracious to us for our past and the way we raised them. They seemed to have taken the good things from our experience and found the best of all their experiences. None of us are in exactly the same place on any issue, but we are all thinking for ourselves and accepting of each other.

Controlling our children into believing like us almost never works out. Our energy is much better spent fostering mercy, love, forgiveness, and compassion for others. It's better to give them analysis tools than to give them what we consider to be treasure.

My daughter that stood over me and told me off was at my house the other day. We sat on the porch with her son and composed some music on her guitar to one of my poems about my dog. It was a beautiful night, and I realized how much I respect her. She is brave, she thinks for herself, and she has found her authentic, vulnerable voice.

Our relationship wouldn't have been the same if I didn't evolve through deconstruction, and the work I have done in my Shadow.[2] Some of my beliefs were toxic, and I needed to be brave and rethink for myself about what was important to me. I have become a much more present and authentic dad and papa.

Laura and I joke that we want to be like our kids at various times in our life. It's true. Most of the things we thought we cared about when they were young turned out to not be that important and only desires of our ego and a fear of what others would think. The good things we are discovering now echo what our children are finding as well. We are on a brave, exciting journey that includes our children. We hardly ever agree totally, but we feel like we have tools of discovery that will lead us all to where we should go.

The only thing we're afraid of is going back to where we came from.

Be where you are, be who you are, be at peace.

PART II: FINDING COMMON GROUND

4

VALIDATING YOUR CHILD'S EMOTIONS

By Laura Forehand

I STARTED TEACHING LATER in life, but I have refined my skills of classroom management to where I always feel like I am in control and moving towards valuable objectives. I teach 2nd grade at a rural elementary school, and although the challenges are varied, they are somewhat predictable. I can usually guess what children will say under most circumstances, and very little surprises me anymore.

But one day when the children were playing with Legos, one of my students blurted out, "I'm stupid."

I pulled him aside and quickly reassured him, "No, you are not."

He defiantly argued that he was sure that he was because someone in his family informed him of that "fact." My heart broke, and I realized I hadn't responded adequately to this young fellow, but we often respond to heart-breaking situations like this the best that we can.

We want to rescue them quickly. We see them in danger, and we need to quickly save them even though their misunderstanding is probably deeply rooted. In this situation, we can't always rescue or even help them immediately. If the person they care about most thinks they are deficient, then they will likely think less of themselves than they should.

While we don't want them to feel these negative emotions, the real problem may be our own discomfort. If our child or our student feels bad about themselves, it reminds us of how we sometimes feel about ourselves or, possibly, how we were treated in our earlier days.

But this young man in my classroom didn't need me to rescue him or tell him the right answer. He already believed the lie propagated by the person he cared about. He may not have wanted it to be true, and he may not have been happy about it, but he believed it because of who told him. What did he need from me that I did not give him?

Before I said anything else, I should have validated how he was feeling. The simplest way to do that is just to repeat what you hear. When he states that he feels stupid, I could have simply said something like, "So, you feel stupid?"

There is no need to agree or disagree with him initially. We are talking about how he feels, not how I perceive the situation. We must acknowledge his feelings and acknowledge where he is emotionally.

When my husband and I are focusing with someone, we often help them say how they are feeling. They will eventually say, "A part of me feels...." After they express how they feel and where they feel it, we don't tell them they should or shouldn't feel that or whether we agree with how they feel. We simply repeat it back to them. We say, "So, a part of you feels..."

We tell them often that they have a right to feel how they feel. Usually, that gets the ball rolling toward healing. We must avoid the urge to respond from our own trauma, which always comes out reactionary.

We can respond to our children in similar ways. We may have greater influence on them, but that makes it even more relevant what we say and how we say it. Often, the pause between our reaction and our response makes all the difference in the world. In just the short time it takes to draw a breath, we can choose more effectively whether to speak or not and what would be best to say.

As I mentioned before, we don't want our children to feel pain, and we desperately try to rescue them from it when we can. I remember when my children experienced physical pain, and I always went to them immediately and did what I could to alleviate it. It is much the same reaction when we see them emotionally hurting.

Our initial reaction may be to rescue them from feelings of unworthiness and find a quick fix to their problems, but often it makes sense to do something a little more deliberate and pursue a more thoughtful approach. Certainly, there are life-threatening situations and that is why we have the basic instinct to act quickly. But most things are not life or death, and they will benefit from a deliberate, thoughtful response.

Initially, my job is not to judge how they feel, but to hear it clearly. The best way to acknowledge how someone feels is to ask directly, "How do you feel?" then repeat their answer back. I was so surprised the first time I did this. It meant so much more than me hurriedly trying to imagine a solution for them.

Most often people and children respond with more information that begins with, "Yeah, and . . ." where they dive deeper into the cause and reason why they feel that way. Given enough time and care, they may even be able to devise their own solution to the way they are feeling without us having to imagine one for them.

Especially with younger children, we may have to help them recognize emotions they have trouble verbalizing. We can say, "Does it feel more like this or more like that?" Even if their answer is as vague as "ucky like," go with the answer they determine is best while continuing to help them with the vocabulary.

I think it is especially important not to presuppose what they are feeling. Many times, my children surprised me in their understanding. They may not have had the vocabulary, but they are the experts at how they are feeling, and they probably think about that more than anything else.

We should take the role of an observer and anything we can do to remind us to stay in that role is helpful. Breathing deeply helps us pause and listen long enough for them to form their next thoughts. We might ask, "How does that make you feel?" or "How do you describe what you are feeling?"

I can't emphasize enough how important it is to pause and make sure you're not giving advice until they have thoroughly explored the depths of what they feel and what they think that feeling is telling them. Listen, ask questions, and breathe.

We don't just get these negative messages from parents; they also come from other groups, including religion. Children gain clarity about their feelings and desires when we verbally reflect them, but other messages and even trauma are being introduced from the messages they are hearing from others.

The best way to penetrate the messaging we all received is to ask, "How do you feel about that?" This helps us understand how they have processed what they have heard and whether it had a positive or negative impact.

Our children have forgiven us for most of the mistakes we made, but it might have been better not to make the mistakes in the first place. I hope you learn to become proficient in pausing after the initial shock so you can respond to your child with better questions, instead of simply reacting. Learning to understand and validate your child's feelings may be one of the superpowers that parents have been searching for.

5

PARENTING THROUGH MODERN CHILD DISCIPLINE AND TRAUMA-INFORMED LENSES

BY CHRISTOPHER & ELIZABETH EAKER

IF YOU ARE READING this book, we suspect you can sympathize with the uncertainty and confusion surrounding parenting while deconstructing. In this chapter, we will discuss some of our history so you can understand how we used to feel about being parents. We will discuss some of the psychology and research-based techniques we have learned and now use - some days better than others! - in dealing with our son's feelings, fears, and behaviors. While we have no clear-cut advice as each family's and child's needs are different, we have learned things we feel have made us be healthier parents. Not surprisingly, we have gone through a spiritual transformation over the last several years which led us to rethink much of what we used to believe about God, the Bible, and therefore, parenting.

This slow evolution coincided with our son's formative years. Parenting through deconstruction is no small feat. Shifting beliefs and philosophies feel like the ground is constantly moving beneath your feet. As beliefs change, so do your ideas about how best to be a parent, what skills are important, and which methods still make sense. Sometimes beliefs change so fast there is no opportunity to find your footing in your new worldview before they shift again. To make it more difficult, beliefs from the past still rear their ugly heads and make you doubt whether you are doing the right thing. What if we fail? What if our son ends up a deadbeat— or worse...an atheist! — because we didn't discipline the "right way" or teach him the "right things" about God? How can he grow up to be a moral man if we are not in church every week, teaching him to study the Bible, or praying as a family daily? These are all questions we've struggled with and, frankly, have no answers to.

Our Background

We are a white, middle-class couple who used to be evangelical. We have one son, Luke, who is in early elementary school. Our upbringing in predomi-nantly white, evangelical, Protestant churches gave us a certain lens through which to view the world. This lens was presented to us as the only right lens through which to view the world. Our churches never talked about the lens but rather spoke about a Biblical worldview. God was sovereign and in control. We were sinful and needed a savior. The Bible was God's word, inerrant and trustworthy in all it says. Through the Bible, we could know what God had chosen to reveal about God's self. If the Bible said God did, said, or acted a certain way, then that was how it was, no debates allowed. We also were raised to believe that the Bible had much to say about how to be a godly parent and raise godly children.

Proverbs was replete with pithy sayings that God intended us to take to heart. "Train up a child in the way he should go, and when he is old, he will not turn from it," was the main guiding principle in parenting a godly child.[1] Proverbs 22:15 encouraged corporal punishment saying, "Foolishness is bound up in the heart of a child; the rod of discipline will remove it far from him." Of course, since God wrote these bits of advice, we were taught they were acceptable and even the *best* way to parent. These were offered to us as timeless truths that God intended us to use no matter how the culture around us changed or how modern child psychology began to promote other techniques of child discipline.

Not surprisingly, our image of God directly affects how we relate to and act towards others, including our children. We become like the god we worship. If the god we worship is angry, we feel the permission to exhibit a righteous anger towards others, which we believe God also feels about that person. If the god we worship is critical, then we will also be critical towards others. If the god we worship excludes, we feel the permission to exclude. The irony is that while we do become like (or mimic) the god we worship, we also make our god in our own image. It is a circular logic: we make our god in our own image then worship the god we made. Humans (especially men, though not exclusively) have a tendency towards being aggressive, hurtful, angry, exclusive, and sectarian. We tend to project these innate tendencies onto God and then believe that is how God is. How this relates to being a parent is that when we believe God expects an impossible standard of righteousness from us, then we as parents project that onto our children. We expect them to live up to an impossible standard of behavior.

Dr. Bradley Jersak says in *A More Christlike Way*, "If we see God as an angry taskmaster, then we never enjoy the love and intimacy of God's house." The churches we grew up in modeled God as the angry taskmaster, so that was how we saw God and thereby modeled as parents. According to Jersak, if that is how we act towards our children, then they will have a hard time enjoying love and intimacy in our homes. We all know too many people who could never live up to the impossible level of perfection set by their earthly fathers and mothers. Do we want our children to enjoy the love and intimacy of our own homes? We believe deep down we all desire that for our children, but our beliefs of God and the Bible can warp what we believe to be the right way to be a parent. We need to meet a more loving, more Christlike God. Once we do, our disciplinary methods and how we relate to our children must necessarily change.

Discipline

When Luke was born, we were still fairly entrenched in the fundamental, evangelical worldview. We each had ideas of what being a parent looked like and which disciplinary methods worked from our families of origin. Elizabeth was raised in a home where discipline was firm and feared. Spankings were painful and plentiful. The children had to walk around on pins and needles so as not to raise Dad's anger. Christopher, on the other hand, was raised in a home where physical discipline, while used, was never excessive. Love always was the dominant force. Later, when we married, we discussed how we would discipline our children and what we would teach them about God, the world, and their place in it. Even though we discussed discipline, it's hard to know exactly how you will be until you're put in that situation. So once our son was born, Christopher believed that being a firm disciplinarian meant sometimes the parent needed to spank, while Elizabeth was much more hesitant. Christopher tried to model the loving, yet firm, correction he knew from his own parents.

As our son grew into the toddler years, Christopher soon realized how "pops" on his son's leg affected both of them. Luke would not only cry, but he would also seem so heartbroken that Dad hit him. These responses impacted Christopher on a deep level, and he eventually realized that physical discipline is not healthy. Meanwhile, Elizabeth was using "time in," in which instead of sending our son to his room alone when he misbehaved, Elizabeth would stay and sit with him in the room. Luke would get the correction while also receiving connection and not feeling isolated.

Moving From Old to New

In many ways, our beliefs were shifting from the faiths of our upbringings, but the beginnings were subtle. We both came to marriage later than typical evangelicals, and we had time to watch other young families navigate parenting. Several friends were trying to do things differently from the authoritarian ways that Elizabeth knew. There was time to watch, wonder, and think about how it could be done differently, without fear, without punishment, though still with healthy boundaries. We watched friends who grew up "trained in the way they should go" according to the white, American, "Biblical" model, ultimately departing from it. We also saw friends who lived loving, moral lives teaching their children to be kind and loving towards others without professing Christianity. Somehow, this Biblical authoritarianism was missing the mark, and we searched for answers.

Our first major shift was letting go of the concept of being born into original sin and needing correction which is taught by most Western, evangelical churches. We made this shift first for ourselves and then were able to extend it to others, including our son. We want to see and celebrate the image of God in people rather than approaching every relationship and interaction with a need to point out and correct flaws. For us, it's no longer about sin- i.e., controlling it, confessing it, or punishing it. It's about modeling loving and compassionate behaviors, recognizing fear responses, and offering love, comfort, and forgiveness. This doesn't mean we don't correct behaviors, but we look to connect rather than punish.

Before we started the deconstruction of our faith, we saw other families in our home church (literally, we met in homes) act with less of a "spare the rod and spoil the child" mindset and more of a "connect, then correct" mindset. Part of this came from families with adopted children, and part of this came from other families who wanted to choose to parent differently from their own fundamentalist upbringing. We saw friends modeling discipline with guidance rather than outright control. One of the things Elizabeth talks about often is "taking the long view." When our son was 3 and 4 years old, doing the things that 3- and 4-year-old children do, it occurred to Elizabeth that she could either focus her attention on perfect behavior from Luke now, or instead focus on how behaviors, experiences, and feelings build upon one another. Ultimately, we want to help Luke grow into the man God made him to be over the course of his life rather than focusing on the image of the "perfect little gentleman" our culture expects right away.

Additional parenting help came through learning about parenting through a trauma-informed lens. We learned terminology for what we were experiencing. One example is emotional dysregulation, or the inability to manage emotional responses within a range of normal reactions. Before learning about this, we simply believed Luke was misbehaving and needed correction. Our old selves would clamp down firmly on the behavior and mete out consequences and discipline. Our old selves would think, "What is wrong with you?" In response to his emotional dysregulation, we would also find ourselves emotionally dysregulated. This would send us into a fight, flight, freeze, or fawn response. In responding to him, we would often do things out of our own state of dysregulation that was not helpful.

But we now know that the best resource our son has to stay within a healthy range of emotional regulation is our own presence and help as parents. Thus, we must be aware of what causes us to enter an emotionally charged state and, as the grown-ups in the room, work to lower our emotional states to a manageable level, so we can in turn help him regulate. Now, when Luke is acting out of a state of emotional dysregulation, we can see this and help him instead of simply being a disciplinarian. Instead of thinking, "What is wrong with you?" our new selves think, "What has happened to you to cause this behavior?" This change of viewpoint helps us to have compassion in the heat of the moment.

Let us assure you that we are still a work in progress. We fail what seems like more times than we succeed, but we work at it each day. You don't have to be a perfect parent, only a "good-enough parent," which one researcher claims means getting it right about half the time.[2] That seems doable.

A technique we learned that helps us all stay calm and regulated is called 1-2-3 Magic from a book of the same name.[3] Before 1-2-3 Magic, getting Luke to stop doing things we didn't want him to do looked like us telling him to stop over and over. This would almost always end up with one of us raising our voice at him which would send him into a downward spiral of emotion. In turn, this would send us all down the spiral. It was not fun for anyone. 1-2-3 Magic teaches parents to calmly count when you want to stop a child's behavior, starting at one. If it continues, count to two, then three. When we reach three, the child must go to their room for a timeout equal to one minute per year of age. It took some practice, but now all it takes is counting to one, sometimes two, and Luke stops the behavior without any of us having to raise our voices. We like it because it clearly defines expectations, boundaries, and consequences, with room for our son to try new things, make mistakes, get connection along with correction and try again. This method cut down on so many emotionally-charged times at our home and helped us have a much more peaceful home.

Conclusion

While parenting during deconstruction is difficult, in some ways it is no more difficult than parenting during any other time. No parent can claim they are experts and parent perfectly all the time. At least during and after deconstructing, parents must be purposeful about what they do because they don't have a rock-solid belief system to fall back on. Since the Bible is not our parenting manual, every decision about how to react, what to teach a child, or what not to teach a child must be considered and weighed against your ever-changing belief system. In all, we believe deconstruction has caused us to be better parents, more in-tune with Luke's needs. If we had to pin our changing parenting priorities on two main things, they would be a new image of God and of the Bible. Getting to know a more loving God makes us more loving, not only to Luke but also to everyone around us. This change in what it means to live out our lives as Christians directly led us to open our home to a single mother and her two children. This situation wasn't easy, but it modeled living the way of Jesus. It taught Luke that love is not easy, but it's what we are called to do. Likewise, shedding the belief that the Bible is inerrant and putting it in a place of more appropriate authority has helped us change long-held, harmful ideas about being parents that were neither helpful nor healthy. We have consequently learned about and embraced modern child psychology-based lenses for fostering Luke's development into the man God has made him to be.

6

WHICH WAY SHOULD WE TRAIN OUR CHILDREN TO GO?

By Josh Lawson

"Train up a child in the way they should go, and when they are old, they won't depart from it." – Proverbs 22:6

MOST OF US ARE familiar with this ancient Jewish proverb. It came down to us through the ages in the canon of scripture. Being the deep-thinking believers that we once were, we were taught to apply the proverb as such:

"You've got to train your kids to be good Christians, which means teaching them the Bible and raising them in church. Parents should lead daily family devotions, have their children memorize scripture, and make sure their little butts are in Sunday school, kids' class, youth group, and VBS every time the church doors open."

That's the evangelical version, as least. Roman Catholics and other high churchgoers might have their kids go through a formal catechism process to ensure a proper grounding in the faith. Either way, the principle is basically the same. Your mileage may vary depending on your specific faith tradition, but this understanding at least reflects the general evangelical flavor with which I'm familiar.

Such theological education was meant to program our kids with a favorable disposition toward our belief system that would increase their chance of being "saved"-or, if you prefer, some other term used to describe the personal conversion experience. Furthermore, it was designed to safeguard them against hostile (i.e., different) worldviews they would inevitably encounter out there in "the world."

But then something happened, not in your kids but in *you*. You started asking difficult questions that challenged your own worldview. With great fear and trembling, you began to deconstruct your belief system. The process was long and harrowing, and it nearly cost you your sanity, but somehow you emerged on the other side in one piece.

You're still a parent, though, or you will be in the future. And you're wondering how in the world you should approach your kids on the subject of faith now that you've given up (in whole or in part) so many of the tenets you once held dear. What does it mean to "train up your children in the way they should go" here on the far side of deconstruction?

Personally, I think it starts with the commitment to teach your kids not what to think but *how* to think. Before continuing, however, I need to preface my thoughts with the following caveat: *I have no idea what I'm doing*.

Yes, you heard me right. I have no idea what I'm doing. Neither do you, by the way, and neither does anyone else. As parents, we're all simply winging it no matter what angle we approach it from. There is no manual on parenting, or else there wouldn't be so many purported manuals in existence. The sheer number of "how-to" parenting books out there demonstrates the shockingly obvious fact that no one really knows how to do this right. We're all just doing the best we can with the tools at our disposal.

So, take a deep breath and give yourself a break. You made mistakes in your evangelical past. You'll make mistakes in your exvangelical future. It's all right. That's life.

It feels good to let yourself be human, doesn't it?

Now, having said that, we can get down to the business of this chapter, which is to consider what it means to teach our kids how to think instead of what to think. In a certain sense, we can't really avoid passing on our own values and beliefs to our children, even if we choose to limit the amount of time we spend consciously speaking about those values and beliefs. After all, our kids learn more from us by the way we act than by the way we talk. The example we set in our daily conduct is the primary teacher of their little minds.

This simple truth is why the common parental admonition to "do as I say and not as I do" is complete garbage. Children will always learn more from our lives than they will from our words. We have to accept and work within the parameters of this sometimes-unfortunate fact of life.

Consequently, if our actions are truly informed by certain genuinely held beliefs, those beliefs will inevitably bleed through in our behavior. Our kids will notice this connection and learn from it, adopting some of our beliefs and practices as their own simply by default. Sociologists refer to this process as *social conditioning*, and there's no escaping it.

Social conditioning is not the same thing as indoctrination, however. Indoctrination is the process of teaching a person to accept a set of beliefs uncritically. Like it or not, this is what is happening in most churches and families on a weekly basis. The problem is not necessarily teaching people to accept certain beliefs but teaching them to do so uncritically.

Regardless of social conditioning, then, there are definite steps we can take to limit the amount of indoctrination our children receive, whether from us or from other people. If your aim is to teach them how to think rather than what to think, it is good to steer them away from indoctrinating elements during their most formative years.

In some cases, this might mean choosing not to attend church anymore, especially if the only available congregations in your town are heavily focused on indoctrinating young minds. Or you may continue to attend church while limiting your kids' exposure to certain ideas they might pick up in Sunday School, kids' class, or youth group. After all, it's much easier to dialogue with your kids about certain things they might have heard while sitting in service with you than it is to engage them on things they learned in a separate setting.

You might think this approach is too controlling, however. You might prefer the social benefit your kids receive from a continuing association with your local church, feeling that the risk of them being exposed to toxic theology is worth the tradeoff. That's fine, too. Either way, regular communication is key to a healthy dynamic. It is imperative that you maintain an open dialogue with your kids about potentially explosive ideas, no matter where they encounter them.

Whatever you do, though, you must always encourage your kids' natural curiosity. Don't squelch their personal journey of discovery by giving them easy answers to difficult questions. Don't pretend to know things you don't know. The best teachers don't just give answers. They facilitate the learning process by providing tools that will strengthen and enhance personal inquiry.

Part of that process includes teaching kids how to come up with their own answers to life's toughest questions. How can you equip them for this exploration? For starters, teach them how to read. Then, show them where to acquire knowledge. Guide them in learning how to navigate the Internet safely and how to discern "fake news" from research-based facts. Instill a conviction in their minds to follow the evidence wherever it leads, regardless of whether or not that evidence agrees with their initial assumptions and preconceptions.

In other words, make it your business to develop your kids' critical thinking skills. Contrary to popular evangelical opinion, critical thinking is not averse to genuine faith. Believe it or not, people can ask, "Did God really say that?" without falling into the devil's clutches.

Your children might not choose to adopt your Christian beliefs, or any of your beliefs, as an adult, however. Are you ok with that possibility? You must be ok with it if you want to teach them how to think rather than what to think. Your mission is to set them up to be successful in becoming their own individual selves, not to make them a carbon copy of yourself, or anyone else for that matter, including —*gasp*— Jesus.

I hope I didn't cross the line with that last thought, but let's be honest. Most of what passes for "deconstruction" these days is simply trading one form of Christian faith for another, typically moving from a socially conservative, theologically evangelical, belief system to one that is more socially liberal and theologically progressive.

For example, you might go from attending church down the road while teaching your kids to believe in penal substitution and eternal punishment to viewing church online, teaching them to believe that that the cross was not about God's wrath and that hell is just a metaphor of unforgiveness.

The problem in such cases is that you are still focused on teaching your kids what to think instead of how to think. You're still indoctrinating them to believe certain things that you personally feel are "right" and "wrong." You might have switched teams, but you're still playing the same game.

Now, this is not to say that certain beliefs aren't more damaging than others. Religious trauma on little minds is real, and as parents we should guard against it. For instance, imagine being told at an early age that you are fundamentally broken, that there was something wrong with you from the day you were born. Imagine being told that unless you agree to look at the world in a specific way and adopt certain beliefs as your own, God will see to it that you literally burn in hell forever. Imagine being taught that you cannot trust your own feelings, needs, and desires and that you must constantly look to external sources of authority for your personal validation.

This is no joke. Some of the stuff that passes for "Christian education" these days could be legitimate grounds for childhood psychological abuse. It's no wonder why so many people stop believing in God and require years of therapy to undo the damage that was done to them growing up in religious circles. If you can't understand this, then that's your problem, not theirs.

But these stark imaginations, real as they are for many people who grew up in the Christian faith, represent the malignant side of religious indoctrination. Most Christian education is admittedly more benign. As long as you're not torturing your kids with nightmarish visions of hellfire and brimstone, I won't dispute your right to take this approach to parenting. Despite the limitations that inevitably arise from religious indoctrination, parents are ultimately responsible for giving children their first framework for life.

Even as you do that, though, you can be intentional about showing your kids how you arrived at your own conclusions and how they can arrive at theirs. If you're unsure about something yourself, you can tell them that, too. Tell them you haven't arrived at an answer for yourself yet, but here is how they can form their own thoughts on the matter. Tell them that they're not obligated to accept your views as their own either way, especially if they can demonstrate a better, more effective path in their own lives.

Take the question of LGBTQIA+ relations, for instance. How to understand and relate to the needs of sexual minority groups has long been a sticking point among evangelical Christians. Depending on where you come from, this might still be something you're wrestling with as part of your religious deconstruction.

Perhaps you've theoretically accepted the truth that these folks are not morally degenerate just because their orientation doesn't match your own (sorry, did I just assume a certain type of reader?), but you're also still in process. Even though you might be a genuinely good-hearted person, you're still wrestling with deeply engrained prejudices against queer people.

Once upon a time, you might have thought that loving queer people meant "tolerating" their civil rights in the public sphere while holding the line of "biblical truth" in the realm of church and family. Now, however, you can see the problematic discrepancies in that position. At the same time, you've still got those nagging prejudices from your own childhood indoctrination to deal with, and you're not sure whether you will ever be entirely free from them.

This chapter isn't about you so much as it is about your children, though. Your kids are coming of age with their own questions about how to love their neighbors as themselves, and their healthy development simply cannot wait on your coming to a new conclusion. Even though your personal understanding has begun to shift (theoretically, at least), you're still plagued by a little voice somewhere deep down in your conservatively formed conscience that says, "What if you're wrong and you end up leading your kids to hell?"

What will you do when your daughter comes out to you with the news that she is bisexual? What will you say when your son is under pressure to betray his closest friend by locker room bullies whose bigotry was formed by Christian parents who taught their kids to "love the sinner, but hate the sin"?

This is just one example of where a new attitude toward parenting on the far side of deconstruction comes in. Specifically, the importance of taking an overall approach that is bent on teaching children how to think rather than what to think. Because the last thing you want to do is be responsible for passing on the uninformed prejudices of a previous generation, especially when those prejudices lead people to inflict actual harm on their neighbors who look, feel, and think differently than them.

So, if religious indoctrination is your jam, then by all means go for it. I won't try to stop you. Just be aware of a few things. First, keep in mind that the views you instill in your kids will set the tone for how they relate to other people for the rest of their lives, for better or for worse. Second, know that the theological ship of their secondhand belief system, no matter how well packaged by you or your pastor, will eventually run aground. And when that happens, their ability to survive the shipwreck will be determined in part by the tools you've given them to think for themselves instead of depending on outside sources of authority.

In short, if you want to help your kids live authentically while avoiding the potential pitfalls of their inevitable "crisis of faith" later in life—one that you know all too well by this point— then I encourage you to err on the side of teaching them how to think rather than what to think. Train them up in the way they should go—the way that aligns with their personal identity as a uniquely beloved child of God—and when they are old, they won't depart from it.

PART III: REMOVING OBSTACLES TO RELATIONSHIPS

7

APOLOGIZING TO YOUR KIDS

By Jonathan Puddle

I RECENTLY BUILT A sauna in my home. I know that probably sounds extravagant but it's a cultural thing. My wife is Finnish, and our family lived there for six years. Sauna is an important part of the bathing ritual, and most Finns have a sauna in their homes. Rather than a spa-like luxury, it is an integral part of life in the cold, dark Nordic nation, and we wanted to continue it after we moved back to Canada. I ripped out an old guest kitchen in the lower portion of our home, demolished the shower beside it, knocked out the wall, and built a brand-new shower and sauna complex. Under ideal conditions, the project could have been completed in a few weeks, but it took me 4 years. I ran out of money halfway through, I injured myself, I burned out...oh, and we became foster parents. And also adopted a rescue dog. And kept our marriage afloat and our kids educated during a pandemic. Life is rarely what we expect it to be.

Creating something beautiful out of an old space is complicated. You don't know what you'll find behind the walls. I came within 1/16" (1 mm to my metric friends) of unknowingly cutting a sewage pipe in half. I had to rethink my plans when I discovered pipes and joists that I couldn't move. Very few parts of the project worked out exactly the way I had planned, but you know what? It's beautiful. And peaceful. It's a calm, quiet, warm oasis in our manic lives, and I built every part of it by hand.

Which reminds me of deconstruction and parenting. Few parts of our lives work out quite like we plan, but faith and parenting seem to really take the cake. I thought I had God and church all figured out, until the very things I believed about God led me away from church. The things I had been taught in church about parenting didn't make sense when I had kids myself. Renovations were needed and having kids in the middle of renovations always makes things crazier.

For our part, we had stopped going to church because it had become a machine demanding more and more of me and caring less and less for how I was actually doing. I was wrestling with how to engage with Scripture and had mostly put the Bible down due to sheer frustration, when we found out we were expecting. We had a son, and he felt like a love-letter from God, an invitation to follow joy and hope in the midst of our spiritual wilderness. Ten months later we somehow got pregnant again. I know roughly how it happened of course...but both our boys were surprises. As they grew, no part of their lives or our parenting worked out the way we thought it would. All the tools we were raised with—spanking, time-outs, and groundings—didn't seem right to us. As we discovered our kids' personalities, we felt the need to adapt and plan around them, rather than force them to contort to our ways. We couldn't square the old models of authority and control with what we were learning about the gracious kindness of God, who suffers long and is slow to anger. We had to find better solutions than behavior control and moralism. All our ideas about parenting, all the ways we had been parented ourselves, found themselves placed on the altar of love and set ablaze. Some of them survived and stuck with us. Some didn't.

One that didn't survive was spanking. I had been raised by gentle, loving parents who were never abusive, but spanking was their primary tool for behavioral correction. I remember being spanked numerous times accompanied by an awkward conversation about how they loved me, and this hurt them more than it hurt me, and so on. The thing is, I suspect those intimate, one-on-one conversations did far more for my behavior than the spanking did. When James, our eldest, was born, we were in the midst of deconstruction and renovation. He caused us to rethink everything we thought we knew about love and dignity and human worth. Concepts like original sin and depravity and wretchedness were challenged as we looked at this beautiful human being, just starting to learn how to live. But I fall back on my defaults, as most of us do, when he started driving me crazy. So, I spanked him...once. He was 3 years old, and I bent him over my knee and slapped his bottom. He immediately stood up, turned around, and slapped me in the face. I was completely shocked. I was at a loss to justify why my behavior was okay, and his was not. My gut said, this tool must go. Admit your mistake and humble yourself.

It wasn't long before we found the work of neuroscientist Dan Siegel and others and learned how devastating it is for a child to experience physical hurt from a person they have attached to as a source of safety and nurture. As our faith remodeling continued, we found ourselves no longer believing in a wrathful, vengeful God but a radically loving Father who brings about righteousness and justice in the world by modeling a higher standard of love and giving us his spirit to make it possible inside of us. What kept sticking out to me was how much that love cost *him*. I had been taught that the one who did the sin was the one who had to pay, but God kept showing me a different way: The one who does the *loving* is the one who pays.

We found ourselves moving from a reactionary, offense-based framework to a proactive, co-suffering, grace-based framework. As we moved away from retributive, angry-god theology, we also moved away from "Spare the rod, spoil the child" practices. The core tenet of which was the importance of apologizing to our children, of humbling ourselves. Of swapping out the violence and control of spanking and other similarly authoritative tools that didn't cost us anything, with the humble path of modeling a costly, co-suffering love. Painfully. Embarrassingly. Haltingly. But faithfully.

The truth is that God gets down on his knees to rescue us, redeem us, and heal us. He comes to earth in frail human form to demonstrate that he will never lift a hand against us. He goes as far as allowing us to murder him to make clear the full extent of his love for us. We are invited to offer that same kind of radical love to our children. We aren't God though. We aren't perfectly loving all of the time, and so we will get it wrong. When we do get it wrong, we are faced with an opportunity: admit our mistake and use it as opportunity to model a better way or flex our authority and double-down on the mistake we just made.

Which brings us back to my sauna project. The heater in a sauna requires ducting for ventilation and significant framing support to take the weight of the unit and the lava rocks. This must all be planned and installed prior to the lining and bench installation, but it wasn't until I had almost finished everything that I discovered I had miscalculated the depth of the benches, and so everything I had planned for the heater was in the wrong place. When I realized this, I was furious. I sat there utterly puzzled that I, a clear DIY genius, had made such a mistake. The temptation to plow ahead—committing myself deeper and deeper to a bad course of action—was intensely strong. Stopping now and fixing the problem would involve cutting through the vapor barrier, repositioning insulation, and installing new studs. Even worse, it would mean admitting that I had screwed up. That was the biggest hurdle—pivoting around my pride. In the long run, I knew that I would regret not changing course and fixing the problem now, so I did what had to be done. It probably only set me back an hour, and when I fastened the heater on the wall a few days later, everything was perfect.

It's so easy to continue a bad course of action when we've already invested so much time in it. When you're five or even 10 minutes into the chaos spiral with your kids, stopping and apologizing for what you've done feels like a bitter pill to swallow. Humbling ourselves is hard. Making an intentional change in the middle of a messy parenting situation is not easy, but it is important. I've lost count of the number of times that I have been half-way through a shouting match with my strong-willed daughter only to pause, realize this is stupid and not helping, and get down on my knees and apologize.

One of the most important lessons we learned through our deconstruction is the importance of visibly admitting that we haven't got it all figured out and accepting that we are people in process. When we rejected the de-facto domination of religious figures and embraced the dynamic wildness of the Holy Spirit, we had to let go of our right to *be right* all the time. Our thin veneer of perfection was punctured. We had to be bold enough to pause in the midst of a pissing match with a stubborn 4-year-old, get on our knees, and serve up grace and humility instead. While difficult and even embarrassing, this humble love seems more like Jesus of Nazareth to us than the rigid, stern, distant deity some of us were raised to fear.

Apologizing to your kids is simple—though not necessarily easy. It involves stopping what you're doing, admitting that it's not working and choosing a better path. Let's imagine you're trying to get one of your kids to bed. They're dragging their heels and won't brush their teeth. One more snack, one more bedtime story...you know the drill. Eventually you lose your cool and snap at them, shouting at them to go and brush their teeth this instant. Depending on their temperament, they yell back at you or burst into tears or run off to their room, slamming the door.

Take a moment to ask yourself, what exactly is the problem here? Is your child exhibiting genuinely destructive behavior or are they simply getting on your nerves? Are they a true danger to your life, or are they simply a danger to your plans to drink Scotch in front of the TV? Disobedient behavior doesn't exist in a vacuum; it always comes in response to some kind of stimuli. Did they have a painful experience at school today? Was one of their siblings unkind to them? Do they just need some extra reassurance right now? All of these can be reasons for dragging their heels about bedtime. Human beings are naturally wired for safety and connection so when kids display behavior that breaks connection and destabilizes their surroundings, something has gone wrong.

Furthering the pattern of destruction and disconnection by yelling, threatening, etc., is not going to help. When our kids give us crap and we yell at them, threaten them, send them to their rooms, etc. we can feel that their actions justify ours. But they should not have that kind of control over us. When they see that their ability to cause distress is greater than their caregiver's ability to withstand it and remain at peace, an additional layer of fear and chaos is added to their world. All these things further destabilize the connection and make future behavioral problems more likely. None of these situations are necessarily your fault as a parent, but it is your responsibility to be the grown up, to maintain your peace and to bring holistic peace to the child and the relationship. I realize that in the heat of the moment this can be difficult, so let's talk a little bit about how the brain works, and then come back to the practice.

The human brain is highly focused on survival and making meaning. It constantly scans the world around us for signs of danger and for clues about why things happen and what they mean. When our bodies sense danger, parts of our brain release chemicals and hormones to move us into action. Our rational, thinking brain goes offline and our animal, survival brain kicks into high gear. When a child feels that they are unsafe or unseen, the fight or flight reflex can be triggered, and they urgently need to find a way to safety and connection. All humans, but especially children, need care and connection. They crave attention and need to know that they are safe. If they feel unsafe or uncared for, they will attempt to interface with you (and other adults) to get the security and love they need. What this often looks like is annoying behavior to try and get our attention and tune in to them. Ironically, we miss—or misinterpret—these signals much of the time. In an ideal scenario, we would recognize bad behavior for what it is—a declaration that a need is not being met—and we would respond with love and care. The trouble is that a child's attempt at connection often comes across as irritating, bothersome behavior, and we don't see it for what it is. We misidentify a tender heart in need of assurance as a misbehaving brat in need of correction, and everyone ends up frustrated.

As adults, our needs are not so different, and our brains work much the same. When our plan for a quiet evening is threatened or our new sofa gets scribbled on with permanent marker, our brains can misinterpret it as a survival-level threat. We move outside our window of peaceful tolerance and enter a state of barely controlled chaos, desperately seeking to find safety for ourselves. Often, our default reaction is to attempt to eradicate the source of stress by controlling, punishing, or banishing the child. When we lash out like this, their brain records that they are not safe, and so their survival instincts are further triggered, and their intensity ratchets up even more. That ratcheting up of their energy makes you feel more threatened also, and so the cycle continues. Before long we're screaming at one another, threatening grounding for life, and generally all behaving immaturely. When adults model this kind of behavior to their kids, it's no wonder that so many children eventually grow up to exhibit similar problems, addictions, and maladaptive behaviors as their parents did. What we model, they repeat.

But there's another option: we can embody mindfulness and humility. We can offer apologies and grace. We can stop fighting fire with fire and instead defuse frustrating situations by meeting their underlying needs and giving care and attention. It's our job to give them the respect and kindness that they need and to make whatever changes in our lives are necessary to ensure we can continue to do so.

So, stop what you're doing. Put down your phone. Go and find the unhappy child and look in their eyes and apologize to them. Own anything you did to ratchet things up further, and don't make any excuses. I don't care if it's not your fault or it's not fair, if you contributed any harm at all, own it: "I'm sorry sweetheart, I shouldn't have raised my voice. I grew impatient, I lost my cool, and I yelled at you. That's not OK and I'm sorry. That's not what a parent should do, I was wrong to yell at you."

When we own our shortcomings and apologize wholeheartedly, we teach our children exactly how a mature person behaves. "I did this. It was wrong. I am sorry." This will go a long way to restoring connection with your child, at which point you can work through the issue at hand. If your child is simply acting up and you need to correct them, it's always better to do so from a place of connection. If your child's behavior is actually not the problem and you're the one who is preoccupied with something that you need to stop, then connection is also the best way to remind you of this and pull you out of your distraction. If no one really has a problem, and it's just a situation of tiredness, fear, etc., then, again, connection and calm is the key. Pivoting your behavior and apologizing wholeheartedly for any ways that you did not respond properly not only models a better way to be. It gives you the chance to clarify your intentions and take a second pass. Spankings and groundings miss out on this second pass.

However, it's worth pointing out that when our apologies include blame for the child, such as "I'm at the end of my rope because you're driving me crazy!", it reveals to our kids that we're not mature enough to be responsible for our own behavior. Again, that's a problem. If you're genuinely unable to remain at peace because of the way your kids trigger you, don't be ashamed. Your needs are valid as well, and you are allowed to pursue your own healing further. I recommend finding a professional therapist who can work through your own childhood trauma or neglect and help you discover your triggers and find wholeness.

By apologizing, we show our kids that apologies are good. We show them that a strong, powerful person owns their mistakes and makes things right. This is the one of the best ways we can raise our kids in lives of love and grace. My prayer is that each of you would find the strength to walk in humility alongside your children. Apologize often, apologize well, and show them what true strength of love looks like. As you move away from dogmatic control, spiritual abuse, and toxic religion, may your parenting also be dynamic, adaptive, kind, and supportive. Just like Jesus.

8

LET THEM BELIEVE

BY DESIMBER ROSE WATTLETON

(Content Warning: Sexual Assault)

IT'S 8:30 A.M., AND I'm standing on a chair in front of a broken clock, staring, trying to make sense of what I see. I haven't been awake for two hours yet, and somehow I've managed to commit two offenses worthy of corporal punishment. That morning I remember proudly telling my mother I was ready for church, and she responded, "You think you're ready?"

I didn't know what she meant by that, but her tone indicated I wasn't. She asked me again as I looked back at her stunned and silent. I began to check myself to see why this had become an interrogation and realized I had not buttoned up my dress in the back and didn't have my shoes on yet. There is black space between the first interrogation and the next...standing on a chair beside my mother, screaming at me to tell her what time it is. She's pointing at the clock so hard that she breaks the glass with her finger. At just five years old, I apparently should be able to tell time...but I couldn't make sense of it. Her next words were, "I've got something for your ass." We all knew what that meant.

As she stormed off to find a belt, I look over to the couch in desperation. All my siblings are sitting, lined up in their Sunday best, staring back at me in fear and sympathy. My eldest sister whispers to me, "It's 8 o'clock," looking petrified at the hallway hoping not to get caught. When my mother returns, belt in hand, she asks me again, "What time is it?" and I answer, barely above a whisper, "It's 8 o'clock." She looks over at the couch because she knows someone helped me, but she can't prove it. I happened to be the target of her rage that day but managed to narrowly escape her wrath. So, off to the Kingdom Hall we go for morning worship.

I was raised a Jehovah's Witness. I didn't really understand what this meant when I was young except to know it meant we couldn't celebrate any holidays or birthdays. It also meant getting up early on Saturday mornings for Field Service, which consisted of getting dressed up to go out and invite people to slam doors in our face. I don't remember what prompted the question, but I remember my mother asking me, "Why do you think we come here?" And I had responded, "We come here to be punished." This was my interpretation of what we like to call fellowship. Being made to dress up, come to church, sit down, be quiet, and by all means, Stay Awake! The penalty for dozing off was being made to sit up on the absolute edge of the seat with a straight back so that if we fell asleep, we would fall off the chair entirely.

If I were interviewed about what it's like to be a Jehovah's Witness at 10 years old, I'm pretty sure my response would've gone something like, "It's boring. I don't understand most of what's happening. I don't have hardly any friends here because most of the people are white and affluent, and we are black and poor." I remember the Elders could barely remember our names and usually got us confused with the kids of the only other black family in the church.

Holidays were especially depressing. Imagine every single Christmas all your friends come back to school talking about the presents they got, and all you can do is listen with a sense of isolation and hopelessness knowing you would never know the feeling of waking up to a tree full of lights and gifts. Every Halloween we were in the house with all the outside lights off, with a sign taped to the door saying, "No Candy," to ward off any devilment of sugar hungry ghosts and goblins that may stop by. Every birthday we got a pat on the back or a hug but not a single solitary gift. Not One. No cake, no party, Nothing. To this day I've never had a birthday party. I'm pretty sure I'm still a bit bitter about that. I would say that as a child, growing up as a Jehovah's Witness seemed like one of the cruelest things you could do to a kid.

Fast-forward a few years and my mother has disassociated herself from the church after a series of incidents with the Elders. I was too young to remember why, but since I've been grown, she has told various stories pertaining to racism and favoritism among other things. So, my brothers, sisters, and I start attending New Light Missionary Baptist Church, where our grandma and all our friends were going. It was a drastic change, and it was actually fun, at first. With children's church, revivals, choir rehearsals, and outings, it was a far cry from the stoic, uniform worship experience of the Kingdom Hall. It wasn't long before the honeymoon was over.

A year into my attendance a new pastor was installed. He had a beautiful wife and young children. His stepdaughter and I became close friends, and it was not long before we were having sleepovers, and our little clique became inseparable. Once again, I found myself being singled out.

This time I was 14 years old and had become the subject of the pastor's affection. Innocent at first, or so it seemed. The special treatment, small gifts, compliments, and hugs. Looking back now I realize how patient his plan was. I was groomed for 4 years. Every year his behavior became more and more inappropriate. Every year my allegiance and affections became more and more loyal. At 18 years old I find myself on my back, in the backseat of his car, looking up at the ceiling as I lost my virginity...to my pastor.

It seems I've had a bullseye on my back tied to church and religion all my life. I have a thousand stories to tell of a life marked and branded by those experiences. As a child, I remember thinking that when I grow up, I would never come back to the Kingdom Hall, and I certainly wouldn't make my children come. I never would've imagined that I would actually grow up and become a pastor. And so there I was, dragging my children to church. Sometimes they wanted to go, sometimes they didn't. The church I pastored was non-denominational, and I wasn't nearly as religious as I was raised to be. So, my children did get to celebrate holidays and birthdays at least. From time to time, they would say, "Do we have to go?" And my answer would be a stern and emphatic, YES. So, until recently, they had been in church all their lives.

It seemed the more involved with the inner workings of ministry I got, the less I wanted to be associated or involved with religion in general. I pastored on and off for about 10 years before a series of unfortunate events nearly caused me to just about lose all faith and patience with the institution of the church itself. I stepped down from pastoring in December 2020, and at that moment, I literally couldn't care at all if I ever attended another service. I felt spiritually, emotionally, and physically drained. Not only did I step out of the pulpit, but I walked away from church entirely. Aside from an occasional visit to support a close friend who was speaking I had all but given up on the idea of regular church attendance. I had seen too much, experienced too much, and knew too much to believe or receive the empty religious rituals, traditions, pomp and circumstance of religious gatherings. Having witnessed wickedness, confusion, chaos, pain, and betrayal from the pew to the pulpit I was simply over it.

What I didn't realize is that the same system I was determined to discard was the same system and structure that framed my children's faith and way of life. At first, they were simply happy they didn't have to get up early on Sundays anymore. Then after a few weeks they began asking about their friends and Sister Debbie. She was one of the sweetest women at the church who always brought them candy. My response to them would be something like, "We're not going today," or "We'll go back to visit sometime." This was my first error.

As a parent, I'm the closest thing to God that my children can experience. They learn to see and hear Him through me. Since the day they were born I had been in ministry. I was pastoring when I became pregnant with my first child and was still pastoring when I had my second child. Both of my children knew nothing but church as a way of life. Their faith and value systems were built in church. Not communicating my decision to them and having that conversation with them was an error on my part. This was an error I wasn't immediately aware of for months.

Up until recently, my decision to step away from church in an effort to define myself beyond my title and get closer to God actually pulled them away from Him...or at least the version of Him they understood. They eventually stopped asking when we were going back. But flickers of their faith and thirst for God surfaced periodically—a thirst that I had deliberately instilled in them and then snatched away without explanation or replacement.

One morning we were headed to school and happened to leave out just as the sun was coming up. My 8-year-old son said, "When are we going back to that morning church?" I asked what morning church? He said, "You know, the one by the water." He was referring to a sunrise Easter service by the lake that one of my friends had invited us to earlier in the year. It was a beautiful, casual service where we worshipped God as the sun rose. There were pastries and cocoa for the kids. We had communion, and my son enjoyed throwing rocks in the water. I told him I didn't know when.

Not long after that my daughter came home from school looking a little down. I ask her what's wrong and my daughter —my 9-year-old daughter— tells me that she's feeling lost. I asked her why she was feeling lost, and she said, "I don't know. I just don't know about life, and like, religion and stuff." I said, "You mean like God?" She said, "Yes like God. I just feel like, I don't know, lost." I don't know what happened that day at school to make her feel lost, but in that moment, I realized my second error.

As a parent, the responsibility I had in helping my children to know and understand God for themselves did not walk away from me when I walked away from the pulpit. My children had quite literally been born into the church, and at just 8 and 9 years old, I had made a decision concerning *My Faith* without factoring *Their Faith* into the equation.

As a parent it is impossible for me to go through deconstruction alone. What may be deconstruction for me proved to be demolition for them. Pulling them out of the church abruptly without explanation was short-sighted and damaging to my children's sense of faith and purpose. It dawned on me that my decision to walk away was based on my life, my knowledge, and my experiences. This decision was 40 years in the making. Everything I had experienced up to that point, and my interpretation of those experiences as it relates to my faith and the institution of religion has brought me to this place, but my children are not here with me. None of these experiences belong to them.

My children don't know what I know. They haven't seen what I've seen. They'll never know what it feels like to be raised by a strict, religious moth-er. They haven't experienced having their innocence manipulated and their world turned upside down at the hands of their pastor. I am the only pastor they've ever known. I now understand that regardless of where I am in my walk with God and my relationship with the church, I am still the shepherd of my children. I still have a God-mandated responsibility to "train them up in the way that they should go," as instructed in Proverbs 22:6. So here I am again, attending church. Not because I believe I need to, but because my children want to, and I take complete responsibility and pride in their desire to know God and experience Him in a way they can understand.

One Sunday we visited four different churches searching for one that had an active and engaging children's ministry. The result was a decent message, pretty good worship music, and a few hours of peace for me, with the kids emerging from children's church with smiles on their faces, excited and eager to tell me what they learned and show me their crafts.

Here's the thing about deconstruction that my children have taught me. Deconstruction is not about shunning all religious institutions, images, or iterations of God and the Gospel. It's about finding a personal path to God that brings peace and purpose to every aspect of your life. It's about shaking off the weight of failed expectations and traumatic experiences and picking up the healing, acceptance, and love of God. It's about resting from the rigor of religion and taking God up on His invitation in Matthew 11:28-30 to "Come unto me, all ye that labor and are heavy laden, and I will give you rest. Take my yoke upon you and learn of me; for I am meek and lowly in heart: and ye shall find rest unto your souls. For my yoke is easy, and my burden is light."

It is because of what I went through growing up in church and in life that I was able to provide a different experience for my children as their mother first, and then their pastor second. There is not yet anything constructed in their life that needs deconstructing. That is a process I must navigate to become stronger in my faith without causing my children to become weaker in theirs. As I evolve toward a greater place of spiritual clarity, I must pursue my purpose without injecting chaos and confusion into the hearts, minds, and souls of my children. I have peace where I am, and they deserve that same peace. I owe it to them to let them experience God in a way that makes sense for them, and to let them grow into their relationship with God on their own terms. They will have an opportunity to decide for themselves how they want to relate to God and faith through their own knowledge and experiences as they become adults. In the meantime, I will offer them opportunities to worship in different environments with different denominations while closely monitoring what is being said, what my children are being fed, and where they are being led. This was my responsibility from the beginning and remains my responsibility now, as a parent in pursuit of purpose and faith by way of deconstruction.

9

LIGHT IN THE DARKNESS: DISCOVERING OUR IDENTITIES SO WE CAN HELP OUR CHILDREN DISCOVER THEIRS

By Ben Delong

I SAT IN THE prayer room of my spiritual director on a cool, spring, Northern California day. Our custom was to meet for coffee and discuss challenging questions over a latte. This meeting demanded more privacy. I sat with tears pouring down my face, weeping from the depths of my being. I had shared frightening thoughts and secrets I never thought I could, and his enduring compassion caught me off guard. I began to discover a truth that I had never really understood, except in the deep recesses of my soul that I forgot even existed.

"The light shines in the darkness and the darkness has not overcome it."[1] John writes this in the epilogue of his Gospel as he speaks of Jesus the Christ and the mystery of the incarnation. What the early church confessed, and what people like Richard Rohr are reminding us of now, is that the incarnation began, not with the birth of Jesus, but in the very beginning of creation. As John also writes in the prologue, "God created everything through him, and nothing was created except through him."[2] Paul echoed this sentiment in Colossians when he wrote, "For in him all things were created: things in heaven and on earth, visible and invisible, whether thrones or powers or rulers or authorities; all things have been created through him and for him."[3]

Nothing in all of creation is devoid of the presence of Christ, and that includes us. We are created in the image of God, as the writer of Genesis puts it. Yet, something even deeper takes place in the incarnation of Jesus Christ. There are so many beautiful passages describing the impact this has one is. Jesus told his disciples, "When I am raised to life again, you will know that I am in my Father, and you are in me, and I am in you."[4]

In Paul's understanding, we were wrapped up in Christ in the incarnation so that what happened to him happened to us, then and now. He describes it in a few different ways.

"For just as through the disobedience of the one man the many were made sinners, so also through the obedience of the one man the many will be made righteous."[5]

"For as in Adam all die, so in Christ all will be made alive."[6]

"My old self has been crucified with Christ. It is no longer I who live, but Christ lives in me."[7]

The light shines in the darkness, and the darkness has not overcome it. Most often Christians think this means that the darkness of sin and death cannot defeat Christ, and of course, this is true. However, the implication is also that the darkness cannot overcome the light of Christ that is within each one of us. We are all wrapped up in the life and love of God.

It sure doesn't feel like that all the time, though. The darkness often feels overwhelming, as if it will swallow us like a giant wave. That's why our instinct is to try and bury it or cast it out of sight. That's what we do with our personal and societal darkness.

It's nothing new. All cultures do it one way or another, often in some form of scapegoating. The culture that Jesus grew up in was no exception. People displaying signs of mental illness were cast out to live in the tombs. Those with physical illnesses were avoided. People with handicaps were believed to be cursed by God. These situations can make us uncomfortable. We don't want to be reminded that the world is often a frightening place where people get sick and bad things happen for no apparent reason, so we formulate ways to keep the darkness at bay.

Jesus clearly didn't play by those rules. He associated with the people that were supposed to be kept in the shadows. He saw the humanity and dignity in them. He often did this at the most confrontational time as well, such as in the middle of the synagogue on the Sabbath, where everyone could see and be perturbed.

This desperate attempt to hide the darkness doesn't just happen at a societal level. We do it in our relationships. We do it in ourselves. We use all kinds of defense mechanisms to avoid having to deal with uncomfortable realities within us. Maybe we are prone to manipulate. Maybe we have a bit of narcissism. Maybe we have scars that are just too frightening to face. We bury all of these. It seems easier.

Jesus doesn't play that game either. He was willing to face the potential darkness within himself: the pain of living as a child whom others viewed as illegitimate, the temptation to give in to despair. Jesus dealt with the same human struggles we do, but by the Spirit, he faced them, all the way to the cross. He wants to help us face our darkness in ourselves so we can see the truth: The light of Christ shines in the darkness, and as much as it might feel to the contrary, the darkness has not overcome it.

I have been on the journey of what many call deconstruction for well over a decade. The catalyst was my realization that my faith wasn't working for me. It wasn't helping me face depression, anxiety, insecurity, or just a general sense that I was worthless. In fact, my faith often made it much worse.

In the Gospels, Jesus demonstrates a pattern that each of us is invited to. It is a pattern of death and resurrection. It is a pattern of letting go of who we thought we were and rising to a new sense of our true identity. This is what I needed from my faith. Jesus' journey to the cross is meant to help us face the darkness in our lives. The problem is that in my church experience, Christians often use the cross as a rug under which to sweep everything that we want to avoid.

The cross is meant to be an invitation to participate in the death and resurrection pattern. After all, Jesus told his followers to take up their own cross, and that only by losing their lives for his sake would they really find them. Unfortunately, the church even finds ways to keep the cross at a distance.

We do this by how we speak of the significance of the cross. Most evangelicals speak of Jesus' death as an event where he took a punishment from a vengeful God that was meant for us. Such a view only took shape about 500 years ago, which is relatively recent in the scope of Church history and would have been completely nonsensical to the early church. In fact, the Eastern Orthodox Church sees this narrative as heretical because of how it portrays the character of God.

If we see the cross as a punishment taken for us, then it doesn't have to have any connection to our everyday lives. It is simply something we can say "thank you" for and be on our way. Thus, Christians speak of taking their burdens to the cross and leaving it there. But the cross is not a depot where we drop off unwanted realities. It is a pattern that shows us how to bear them as Jesus bore the cross so we can go deep into the darkness and find what it conceals.

Of course, this view of the cross is possible because of the vengeful and sadistic patterns we attribute to God. If that is who God is, then it is no wonder we don't want to get too close. This leaves us with a dilemma. We don't want to face our darkness, but we also don't want to face a hateful God.

That leaves us with little choice but to grind out our days, doing the best we can to stay afloat, and wondering why we are miserable.

That is not what Jesus' Abba desires for us. As parents, that is not what we desire for our children either. They need someone to help them face the darkness, to sit with them in it, and we can only do that if we've faced it in ourselves. We can only lead them where we have been.

The evangelical Gospel I was given didn't give me a way to do that. It focused on guilt and forgiveness. Those are both two important realities. There are times we feel guilty for doing things that are beneath who we truly are. Guilt is fitting in those moments, as is the forgiveness that is freely offered. A Gospel that stops there, however, is not able to give us all that we need.

Guilt and forgiveness tend to be the focus in most of western Christianity. Guilt is one aspect of sin, and a rather small aspect at that. It focuses on a legal concept of salvation. The early church, as well as the Eastern church today, conceives of sin as an illness that needs healing. The things that we talk about as sin-specific hurtful or immoral behaviors are in fact symptoms of the illness that sin really is. That illness stems from a distortion of our identities. It is believing a lie about who we are and then acting on it. This usually leads to dysfunctional behaviors and defense mechanisms that cause us pain and hurt people around us.

In short, there are reasons we do what we do. There is also a reason our kids do what they do. If we don't go into the darkness, we won't discover what those reasons in us, nor can we help our children with theirs. I had to discover the reason why I did what I did, and I needed a compassionate God to help me.

I grew up in the church as a pastor's kid. While there are many blessings I've enjoyed from that background, the reality was that church life was often extremely dysfunctional. Part of this was due to unrealistic expectations that churches place on their pastors. My father was not equipped for that. He is also part of a generation that doesn't generally seek help for the emotional and mental afflictions such situations can cause.

Another part of the church dysfunction was the Gospel we were taught. We were told we were intrinsically tarnished with sin, and God apparently had an anger problem. Living in that dynamic day after day, year after year, caused a lot of damage to my emotional and spiritual health, as well as to my nervous system. I coped by becoming the most effective people pleaser I could be.

This worked for a time, especially in the church. Churches love people pleasers. Churches are often unable to distinguish between good Christian behavior and unhealthy coping mechanisms. When such mechanisms benefit the church, they sometimes simply don't want to distinguish between them. That's why, if they aren't careful, religious environments can encourage people in their harmful patterns rather than helping them see the deeper issues.

Eventually, my survival techniques hurt more than they helped. This especially occurred after I married my wife. Everything I had done to make it in the world was suddenly backfiring and hurting our relationship, and I had to acknowledge that.

This reality became more pronounced as we sought to become parents. My wife and I became foster parents five years ago. We have had four children come through our home, one of whom we were so blessed to adopt. As we sought to love these children in their struggles and pain, my own demons screamed all the louder. I didn't know how to face their darkness because I was still struggling to face my own.

As I did, I learned the reasons behind my behaviors and dysfunctions, and with the help of so many beautiful people, I have found much healing and empowerment. I've learned compassion for those parts of myself I used to ignore. With this has come a greater empathy for my son. When he is driving me nuts, and I just want to silence the uncomfortable emotions that are pouring out of him, I am quickly growing to understand that there is something deeper going on within him, because I know there is for me too. I've learned that the light shines in his darkness, and I can sincerely profess to him that the darkness has not, and will not, overcome it.

This journey has helped me hold myself to a higher standard that matches my true identity. Obedience and faithfulness flow out of love and identity, not the other way around. That's what so many church environments completely butcher—a reality that I have been complicit in as well.

I can hold my son to a high standard, not because my love is dependent on it, but because it will not let him settle for anything less than who he truly is. Thankfully, he does the same for me.

We have the light of Christ within us, the darkness will not overcome it, and a trip into the darkness is paradoxically the only thing that will show us how true this is. It's a journey worth taking, not only for ourselves, but also for the little ones who look up to us. As they observe us, may they see an empowerment that fills them with hope and courage, and may we all experience the reality of Christ's unending kindness through it all.

10

METAMORPHOSING ALONE: RELATIONSHIP GUIDANCE FOR INTRAFAITH PARTNERS

By Dr. Mark Karris

REMEMBER WHISPERING SWEET NOTHINGS to the person you thought was going to be your Christian soulmate for life? Remember clasping clammy hands with that person, feeling as if the divine bliss you felt would never end? Did you take long walks where magical breezes gently caressed your faces on quiet spring mornings? Sure, there were occasional arguments and disagreements, but that didn't matter because you just knew that God Himself had brought the two of you together and so that didn't matter. Knowing that you were securely home—in *your* community, with *your* God, with *your* God-ordained spouse, with *your* beliefs, and with *your* religious rituals—gave you a profound sense of comfort and safety. It seemed this would go on forever!

And then one day you found yourself catapulted into the Deconstruction/Reconstruction (D/R) journey with a case of *Religious Disorientation Growth Syndrome* (RDGS). The D/R journey is shorthand for those who are going through a seismic shift in their religious and spiritual orientation. Of course, most people change *some* religious beliefs to a certain extent throughout the course of their lives. They may also experience some spiritual growing pains along the way. However, the D/R season is so palpable that many experience a profound sense of disorientation when they find themselves changing. I've designated the cluster of signs and symptoms of this disorientation *Religious Disorientation Growth Syndrome* (RDGS), including:

1. Doubting or denying one's religious beliefs that were once strongly maintained.

2. Subtle or intense anxiety about one's relationship with God.

3. An increase in painful emotions such as anger, loneliness, shame, guilt, sadness, and despair.

4. Isolation and criticism (feared or realized) from members within one's own family and/or religious community.

5. Existential angst concerning one's identity and future self.

RDGS causes people to suffer emotionally, spiritually, and even *physically* for more days than they care to experience. And, paradoxically, this season of disorientation can be a powerful catalyst that leads to colossal emotional, mental, and spiritual *growth*. Though unpleasant, to say the least, I have witnessed many people experience profound transformation after traveling wisely through their D/R journey.

As stressful as the D/R journey itself can be, all the anxiety, fear, shame, and pain magnify exponentially when your partner is in a different religious place than you are, and you walk this unfamiliar pathway alone. While no two people's expeditions across the vast D/R terrain are the same, the one who finds their partner on a similar journey may find some solace in companionship. There can be tremendous comfort in traversing the D/R journey with a loving and safe significant other who is going through the same confusion, loss, and sense of freedom you may be experiencing (though this *sense of freedom* may depend on how far along one is on the journey). However, the person whose spouse is in a different space and place in their spiritual life can sometimes provoke anxiety for the spouse who is *deconstructing* or *reconstructing* long-held beliefs and practices. This can bring about a season filled with intense fear, guilt, perpetual conflict, and a nagging sense of aloneness that feels unbearable at times—or as if you are from two different religious planets!

When you are trying to navigate the D/R journey and are no longer a united front with your partner, parenting can become particularly challenging. Parenting may become a scary minefield as you feel a newfound desire for your children to grow up without the toxic religious ideology that caused *you* childhood suffering, yet your partner still values those doctrinal structures. My hope is that this chapter will offer support and encouragement to the person whose partner is not on the D/R journey, as you might be. May what follows help you become more centered and confident so that you can also be the best partner and parent possible.

Normalize the Kaleidoscopic Metamorphosis

Can you imagine if a caterpillar had an astute mind, intense feelings, and the ability to voice their concerns like we do? I expect that, on the road to mayhemic metamorphosis from crawling insect to majestic butterfly, they would totally freak out! They would fear the absolute worst and drop some serious "F-bombs." Their guttural groans would be heard by many around them, calling their sanity into question. All this before their conscious mind could even realize what had just taken place in them—*complete transformation!*

No one wakes up and excitedly tells themselves: *Today is the day I want to start unraveling my faith, casting myself into the throes of social rejection, despair, and one of the most painful seasons of my life.* But sometimes, before we know it, spiritual metamorphosis thrusts us onto the D/R journey. At one point we are fine, crawling our way around snugly and smugly in a comfortably familiar world. Then, by what mechanism we know not, we step into new territory, become painfully disoriented, and appear "unrecognizable" to those around us. Still, we keep moving forward and, before we know it, we are soaring on a beautiful tapestry of new wings, laced with the vibrant colors of our newfound beliefs—ones more congruent with who we really are. Suddenly we understand it: we've grown. Still, the process of growing was certainly chaotic and confusing!

I encourage you to normalize the kaleidoscopic nature of this journey of metamorphosis. Research shows that when you *name your emotions,* you can tame and normalize your experience, gain a slight sense of control, and feel a greater sense of calm. Like many before you, you are going through (or have gone through) a profound shift that has catapulted you into a season of doubt, anxiety-provoking and painful social realities, existential and identity concerns. On top of this D/R anguish, add the distressing mental chatter inside you about whether your primary relationship will endure such sweeping change in you—and anxiety around how to raise emotionally and spiritually healthy children. Well, these can take your metamorphosis detour to an even higher level of internal chaos.

Your struggle is real. It is normal. Of course, you will experience anger from others as you grow (due to the poison of various elements of Christian principles, practices, policies, and attitudes that have been detrimental to your well-being—*and maybe even your children's*). You will also experience grief and a sense of loss. The reality is that you may lose friends, family, rituals, beliefs, and an identity that was once important to you. You may feel fear that your love relationship will not weather your new faith shift. Or fear that you will always have a "walking on a waterbed" feeling when it comes to your faith, instead "standing on solid ground."

You may feel anxious and not exactly sure how to raise your kids with a robust spirituality that makes sense. You may even experience a sense of euphoric relief and joy, feeling and knowing that your soul is being liberated. One minute you are having positive thoughts about it all. The next minute you are thinking *the end is nigh.*

Let me assure you, you are not crazy. You are not in cahoots with the devil. All the above is normal. Disorientation and a wild ride of conflicting thoughts and emotions is a necessary aspect of the change process toward emotional, spiritual, relational, and parental transformation.

Respond Rather Than React

I remember a time when my wife and I were fighting. It was a difficult season in our relationship. Something I said had triggered my wife, and then out came these words from her: "I don't even know if I want to be with you. We don't even believe the same things. You are a liberal. You don't believe the Bible, and my parents think you are a heretic. We are just too different."

In that moment, I felt like saying something hurtful. I wanted to harshly judge her fundamentalist religion. I also wanted to go into a philosophical and theological tirade on the biblical understanding of what it means to "believe" and how orthodoxy and orthopraxy are inseparable. But instead of *reacting*, I chose to *respond* with vulnerability. I shared with her in a soft and slow manner: "What you are saying hurts me deeply right now. I don't need to believe the same things as you. I don't need for you to believe *exactly* the same as me. Our love is deeper than that."

Before you get the impression that I am always so Zen and Jesus-y, trust me, I am not. There are plenty of times in the past when I reacted, rather than responded. However, effective communication is my heart's intent. I have persistently worked to hone effective communication skills in my relationships. I came up with this rhyme to help me internalize the *react-or-respond* relational principle: "*To keep your relationships intact, it is better to respond rather than to react.*" The late Holocaust survivor, speaker, and author Viktor Frankl stated it better "Between stimulus and response, there is a space. In that space is our power to choose our response. In our response lies our growth and our freedom."

I am talking about reacting and responding because I know how difficult it can be when you and your partner are not on the same page in life stories. It is easy to become polarized with the person you love, especially when you vastly disagree on matters of faith. And when children's hearts and minds are at stake, love can easily turn into war.

War is a proper term when two people conflict with each other. We all have brains that are geared for battle, at least from a neuroscience perspective. We are designed with a nervous system that is constantly ready for fight, flight, freeze, or fawn. Therefore, it is natural for us to defend ourselves and go into *battle mode* when someone treats us unfairly or comes at us with such hard and hot emotions as anger and rage.

You have heard of "free will." I am inviting you to practice "free won't"—the ability to choose *not* to believe or act in a particular manner. It is the ability to choose to respond, rather than to react on primal instincts. Proverbs 15:1 states, "A gentle (tender or soft) answer turns away wrath (anger/fury), but a harsh word stirs up anger." The tone and pace of our conversations (otherwise known as prosody), have a huge part to play in the outcomes of our conversations. Thus, these things impact our feeling of connection with or disconnection from each other.

Research by The Gottman Institute shows that when people start a conversation harshly or reactively it has a 96 percent chance of going nowhere (this is called a *harsh startup*).[1] Why? Because reactivity promotes reactivity and vulnerability promotes vulnerability. We can either trigger the other person's *defense* system with hard and hot emotions or trigger their vulnerable and soft, warm emotions (*tend and befriend* system). I am reminded of what the wise mystic wrote in 1 Peter 3:9: "Do not repay evil with evil or insult with insult, but with blessing, because to this you were called, so that you may inherit a blessing."

Choose your responses wisely. While there is no guarantee that vulnerability will lead to a positive outcome, there *is* a guarantee that a harsh tone and biting words will lead to a conversation going nowhere. So, share your thoughts, feelings, and needs vulnerably in a soft and slow way, and watch your relationship grow day after day.

Get Out of the Fight and Into the Light!

If you start talking with your partner and things get heated, a negative cycle can start to escalate. When this happens, ask your partner for a "time out to go to a *time inward*. Take around twenty minutes apart to self-soothe and brainstorm solutions within, and then go back to a *time-in* to reconnect with your partner. Here are some signs that a negative connecting cycle is starting to take over. One or both of you begin:

- Yelling or getting louder as you speak.

- Having constant negative thoughts about the other.

- Slamming doors or throwing things.

- Not listening to what the other is saying.

- Cursing or using other hurtful language.

- Experiencing muscles getting tense and stomach upset.

If you experience the negative cycle starting to take over, then you can strategize and develop a plan. Be sure you and your partner are clear about the following:

- Who is leaving and where are they planning on going?

- How long will the time out last (Fifteen minutes? One hour?)?

- When and where you will get back together to try discussing the topic again?

- The partner who is leaving is not abandoning the other person but is leaving to center themselves.

The idea is to keep the relationship intact and to keep the conflict from escalating. So, it may be wise to take some time to calm down so that both of you can come back to the discussion as *self-at-best*, not *self-at-worst*.

The purpose of a time out is not only to calm down, but also to reflect on how you may have contributed, even in a small way, to the negative cycle. Additionally, the task to consider what strategy you can engage in now to repair the rupture in the relational bond, if possible. I love what David, the lyricist and musician, wrote in Psalm 139:23–24: "Search me, O God, and know my heart; test [examine] me and know my anxious [troubled] thoughts. See if there is any offensive [*oseb* in Hebrew—meaning "area of pain"] way in me and lead me in the way everlasting."

Instead of praying, "Search me, O God," some people's prayers sound more like, "Smite them, O God! Fix their stubborn heart, and please let them know that they are deeply troubled and have got some serious issues. See their offensive ways, firmly discipline them, and lead them in the way everlasting." OK, I am being funny. However, I might not be too far off here. Instead of blaming your partner and ruminating on how horrible they are, we are encouraged to *keep it real* in prayer. We are invited to ask the Spirit of love to shine Her loving light into the chasms of our hearts. As we co-regulate with God, we can move towards co-regulation and connection with our partner.

If prayer isn't your thing (or you are currently on a hiatus with God) you can also:

- Meditate or listen to music.

- Engage in yoga or relaxation techniques.

- Exercise, or go for a walk.

- Write a letter to "vent" your feelings and then throw it away. Or write a letter and give it to your partner at a later time.

- Call a trusted friend who has the relationship's best interest in mind.

The Lifeline of Self-Compassion

One of the best ways to deal with the stress of working through your spiritual metamorphosis is to practice being kind toward yourself. Self-kindness in the form of self-compassion will be instrumental in your process of exploration, grief, cacophonous emotions, and marital and parental adventures. However, if your Christian journey was anything like mine has been, filled with repeated *original sin, hell-bound* theology talk, then self-compassion may sound foreign to Christian vernacular. When was the last time you heard a sermon with a title like "Three Biblical Principles on Loving Yourself Well"...*never?* For those of us who didn't have adequate teaching and modeling around self-compassion, it may take some practice getting the hang of it.

Self-compassion is not some woo-woo, feel-good psychobabble with no substance. It is a heavily researched topic with tremendous benefits. Self-compassion, as operationalized by the renowned self-compassion researcher Kristin Neff, is a manner of relating to oneself with tenderness and kindness amid suffering or failure. She describes self-compassion in a very practical way: Respond to yourself in times of struggle as you would a dear friend. Self-compassion is correlated with a low incidence of depression, anger, self-criticism, rumination, and other negative effects, as well as an increase in emotional intelligence, positive coping skills, overall wellbeing, social connectedness, life satisfaction, and interpersonal effectiveness.

The research has shown that self-compassion has three core components: self-kindness, common humanity, and mindfulness. Each core component has a counterpart: *self-kindness* is related to self-judgment, *common humanity* is related to perceived isolation, and *mindfulness* is related to overidentification.

Self-kindness involves treating oneself with warmth and compassion during adversity and suffering, as opposed to being harsh to and belittling oneself at a time of difficulty or failure. Common humanity involves recognizing the universal tendency for humans to be flawed, imperfect, and prone to making mistakes. The counterpart to common humanity is the proclivity to isolate oneself and imagine oneself to be the only person going through a particular experience or event.

Finally, mindfulness is one's experience of the present moment. It is the ability to have a balanced view of painful emotions and difficult experiences. The counterpart to mindfulness is overly identifying with negative thoughts or feelings, which involves inflexibility and fusing with these adverse feelings. During your spiritual metamorphosis, you have the option to relate to yourself as the Father of Love relates to you, or as the Father of Lies relates to you. *Do I need to tell you which option is best?*

The Father of Lies is another way of describing the internalized harsh and critical *other* we have within us that whispers daily, "You're a heretic. You and your children's future are doomed!" It is the internal and oppressive wagging finger. The *other* can have deep roots in being raised by cold, distant, perfectionist parents. The authoritarian critical other can also emerge out of larger systemic, oppressive, and dehumanizing cultural dynamics. It can even be the result of church leaders passing down a deformed image of a critical and punishing God that should never have been taught in the first place. Relating to yourself like the Father of Lies means you internalize negative external messages and believe them as though they were your own original thoughts and therefore factual.

Relating to yourself like the Father of Love (or Mother of Love if you prefer) during spiritual, emotional, and everyday struggles is the ultimate goal. In the parable of the Prodigal Son (Luke 15:11–32), Jesus gives us his internal image of the Divine as a powerful, compassionate, loving, and motherly Father, who embodies the best of both masculine and feminine traits. The father in the Prodigal story is a concerned dad who obsesses over his wayward son and who is constantly longing and looking for him. He is a dad who defied cultural gender norms as he picks up his robe, runs toward his son, and then firmly hugs and warmly kisses him.

Instead of giving his son a history lesson on what he has done wrong or scolding him in public, which would invariably have pushed the son further down into a pit of shame and despair, the father reminds him of his true identity. The father gives him royal garb and proclaims boldly, "For this *son* of mine . . .".[2] Lastly, the father knows intuitively that his son needs a coat, slippers, and a ring. The invitation is to treat yourself with similar compassion as you continue your journey of exploration and discovery. Engage in self-compassion:

- When you are struggling with doubts about God.

- When shame and self-criticism whisper in your ear.

- When you lose your temper with your children.

- When you struggle with how to talk about God with your kids.

- When the *tenacious tango* keeps overtaking you and your spouse.

- When family and friends distance themselves from you.

- When you must make the toughest decisions of your life, and it is agonizing.

What does self-compassion look like? It can look like taking a moment to pause during a really stressful day, closing your eyes, putting your hands on your heart, and saying to yourself, *This is a moment of suffering (mindfulness). Many people suffer with relational issues and struggle with raising the beautiful chaos that is children (common humanity). May I be kind to myself in this moment. May I be strong and find the courage to live bravely (self-kindness).*

Another practice is to speak to yourself with more kindness in your internal dialogue. You've probably realized by now that it's easy to be hard on yourself in spiritual metamorphosis. You might speak to yourself by criticizing your own emotional condition, judging your level of parenting skills, bashing yourself for not winning the spouse of the year award—and the list goes on. Say things to yourself that are encouraging, that are going to build you up and will not tear you down. If you can't picture a loving and compassionate God saying it, or if it isn't something you would say to your dearest friend, then don't say the words to yourself![3]

Live Your Values

Russ Harris, an author of many self-help books and a world-wide trainer of "Acceptance and Commitment Therapy" (ACT) often mentions the "Two Kids in the Car" metaphor. I will put my own spin on it. Imagine there are two kids in the back of an SUV, off to Universal Studios! It's a four-hour trip to get there. One kid is completely obsessing about the goal: Every ten minutes he's like, "Mom, are we there yet? Dad, are we there yet? Guys, are we there yet?" The kid is completely impatient, frustrated, and is just wanting to reach his goal. Now, the other kid has the same goal: She wants to arrive at Universal Studios! But she's also in tune with her values of curiosity, being present, playfulness, and having fun. So, she's peeking out the window noticing the different cloud shapes in the sky, giggling as she is waving to other people in their cars, and moving her hips to the boring but tolerable music her parents are playing on the radio. She is engaged in values-guided action while enjoying the journey.

Both kids arrived at Universal Studios at the same time. They both felt the sheer excitement and anticipation of all the glorious things they would experience. But the daughter also had a rewarding journey. *Why?* Because she was not merely focused on the goal but was also living her values.

I know countless people who are stuck on the D/R journey and pressing pause on their lives, because they think they don't have all the right answers. They are constantly asking something to the effect of, *What am I supposed to do while I don't have the theological answers to all my questions.* It is like the "Are we almost there yet?" question. They have convinced themselves that the fruits of this new spiritual metamorphosis, a life they are continuing to piece together, can't blossom until they have *all* the answers to their questions. In their minds, they must spend countless hours deconstructing every theological morsel they remember from their past while critically evaluating each new morsel that presents itself. Unfortunately, analysis can lead to paralysis. A person can have an active mind but live a passive and paralyzed life. This is where knowing and living our values can be so liberating.

Values are words that signify the chosen way we want to engage with ourselves and with those around us. Values are what we want to stand for in the world. They are our inner compass. What we would want to hear our friends and loved ones say about us at our funeral is a good indication of the nature of our values.

Values are not goals. While goals can be attained, values cannot. Values *guide* us as we work to achieve our goals and experience a meaningful life. And, hopefully, they prevent us from living a life that robs us from the experience of healthy connections and divine success.

Have you ever taken the time to name and label your own values? If not, you really should. To jumpstart your own time of reflection, below are some examples from my previous book *Religious Refugees: (De)Constructing Toward Spiritual and Emotional Healing*[4]:

- Acceptance/Self-Acceptance: to be accepting of yourself and others.

- Authenticity: to be genuine and real with yourself and others.

- Spiritual: to connect with that which is transcendent.

- Love: to take actions that put another's interests and desires above your own.

- Gratitude: to express appreciation for the people and experiences in your life.

- Justice: to advocate for and support those who are oppressed and marginalized.

- Curiosity: to ask questions with the intention of discovering answers that provide understanding.

- Adventurousness: willingness to take risks and explore new experiences.

- Cooperation: to partner with others toward common goals.

- Forgiveness: to acknowledge a wrong done to you by yourself or another but demand no further punishment nor harbor further ill-will related to that offense.

- Courage: to act to achieve a goal in the face of threat or difficulty.

- Honesty: to speak truthfully and completely.

- Integrity: to act in accordance with your values in private as well as public.

- Self-Control: to exercise restraint over desires to act against your values.

- Patience: to wait for a desired goal without a sense of entitlement.

- Persistence: to continue to act towards a goal in the face of obstacles or fatigue.

- Kindness: to treat others in a gentle manner that pleases them.

- Humility: to act without the need or desire for praise or recognition from others.

- Transparency: to open your actions to the visibility and scrutiny of others.

- Safety: to provide an environment sheltered from threats to your person or that of others.

- Community: to belong to a group with similar beliefs, values, behaviors, and interests.

Do you see some of your own core values on that list? Which ones take precedence in your life? What are your top five? What values do you have that weren't on the list? During your spiritual metamorphosis, which can be a roller coaster of ups and downs, it is important to know what your values are. Your feelings and moods can change. Your active thought-spitter, otherwise known as your brain, can get stuck in the past or worry about the future. Once you identify and prioritize your values, they become anchors that help you navigate the stormy emotional and mental sea of ideas vying for your attention. Despite not knowing what is going to happen with your marriage, or knowing exactly what you believe, or what, precisely, you will teach your children about metaphysical theological realities, values help ensure that you live a life worth living in the present. After all, the present is all that we have. *Let's live in it!*

Calling it Quits

Jennifer had spent twenty years of her life with Sean. They were conservative, God-loving and churchgoing folks. They had three beautiful children. While over the years they'd had their ups and downs, they were deeply committed to each other and their family. Then, Jennifer's conservative beliefs started to unravel. She could not continue to deny, suppress, and repress her doubts, troublesome questions, and piercing splinters of toxic beliefs.

Jennifer had love and appreciation for friends who were members of the LGBTQIA+ community. Sean, however, was always railing against them. Jennifer started to feel deeply saddened by the ways the church had treated them. The final straw for her was the cognitive dissonance that came about due to observing her pastor and religious family members actively support politicians who acted in ways and shared viewpoints that were in complete contradiction to Jesus' way of life. After a while, she could no longer keep her struggles private. She told her husband about her internal process, and all hell broke loose (metaphorically, and for *her*, literally).

The fights between Jennifer and Sean were terrible. There were plenty of harsh startups. Jeff thought that Jennifer was being led astray by Satan. He believed that she was being enticed by doctrines of demons. They were caught in a vitriolic negative dance. Their pernicious pattern was a repeated sequence of events fueled by negative emotion, initially outside of their conscious awareness, that continually got in the way of intimacy and connection. The more Sean criticized Jennifer, the more she would defend and fight back. The more she shot her verbal arrows, the more Sean increased his verbal bullets. And around and around they went in an attack/attack pattern. Their relationship became toxic, and that toxicity was spilling out onto the kids. To make a long story short, after one year of nothing changing, Jennifer divorced Sean.

I am a hopeless romantic. I am also a therapist who tries to save marriages on a weekly basis (with marked success). However, divorce is a reality. Relationships do not always last. Sometimes two people grow considerably apart. What is worse, over time some relationships can feel perpetually toxic. And worse still is that constant parental discord and relational toxicity can create fear and loyalty binds for the children to such extent that it becomes more harmful for the kids for their parents to stay together rather than divorce.

I am not encouraging divorce. I am also not demonizing it and considering it the unpardonable sin. I want to encourage you to fight for love and see if there can be unity amongst diversity. I would love for you to go to couples' therapy with a trained clinician who specializes in the most empirically validated form of couples therapy, which currently is *Emotionally Focused Therapy* (EFT). I would love for you both to work extremely hard and learn how to be accessible, responsive, and engaged with each other, despite your differences. Your children deserve to have parents who give it their all. And even after you have given it your all, it may not be enough. Sometimes, as messy and painful as divorce can be, the dissolution of the marriage can be the healthier option for all.

Let Love Rule

For some religious folks, feelings of internal unraveling give rise to the powder keg of narcissistic rage when their ideals and doctrines are not mirrored back to them. Narcissistic rage is the signal that a person's sense of self has been unconsciously threatened with fragmentation due to a failure of imperfect mirroring messages from another person. If a spouse becomes aggressive, lashes out verbally, or attacks another physically because their beliefs are challenged, then we are dealing with dynamics that transcend the righteously indignant, "My anger is due to a love for God's Word." It is no longer about "God's Word" or "love." It is about unconscious, egotistical, self-preservation.

For example, take a partner who becomes profoundly angry because their spouse doesn't believe in hell any longer. In their anger, they start to demean and devalue their partner. They may feel and react that way because—on a subconscious level—their illusory identity is built around beliefs that a fragile and fragmented self is jeopardized by your expression of differentness. Their identity is fused with their beliefs.

If a partner challenges their spouse's beliefs, they may be unknowingly challenging their spouse's identity. Their narcissistic wounding, hidden behind the veil of a "love for the Bible," gets triggered. Then, the *fight–or–flight* area of the brain becomes activated, and they protect themselves by lashing out aggressively. Love doesn't harm. Love is patient, kind, is not arrogant and rude, and seeks to connect and heal. Fear and rage divide people into *"us* and *them"* and cause disconnection and harm.

Love Those Who are Different

The Israelites were once an oppressed people in Egypt. And once they became free, they turned around and oppressed, enslaved, and annihilated others, all in the name of God, in order to steal their land. They were a perfect example of the fact that hurt and traumatized people tend to hurt and traumatize others. There is a sad irony in the oppressed becoming the oppressor, the victim becoming the victimizer, and the former fundamentalist—pretending to be free from the constraints of toxic religion—becoming fundamental-*ish*.

Fundamental-ish people are those with sacrosanct religious beliefs who take a prideful, narcissistic, and exclusivist stance that dehumanizes others out of fear. There is a difference between attacking people and attacking ideas. Unfortunately, I have seen far too many "woke" people become free from toxic religion only to attack others for not believing the way they do. We can fight our spouses' oppressive doctrines with our own robust values and firm action. We can love our spouse, even when we find their ideas and actions repulsive. We can be passionate about what we believe, calling out injustice when we see it, and at the same time view our spouse as created in the image of God.

I made a vow not to allow unseen metaphysical realities to get in the way of my relationship with my wife. I don't need her to believe the same things I do. She doesn't have to wrestle with the intricacies of *atonement theories* to be sexy to me. She has many incredible values and qualities that I absolutely love about her, and for which I feel tremendously grateful. I am me and she is she. We are different. That is OK. Love allows for difference, especially with doctrines around metaphysical realities and theories that are mysteries to us all.

Love is Fierce

The *yin* form of love seeks to nurture, connect, and heal. The *yang* form of love is fierce, energetic, and seeks to right wrongs. There may be times when we are propelled out of righteous yang love with a hint of anger to make unjust things right. This is different than anger coming from narcissism and a fragile ego.

There may be times when you need to talk to your spouse lovingly but firmly about doctrines that you feel can cause psychological harm to your children. When it comes to ideas about metaphysical realities that we can't see, I think we can agree to disagree. For example, I can amicably disagree with my wife on the Trinity, or the afterlife, or on matters of salvation (once again, metaphysical realities we can't observe or measure). However, you better believe that I will have that energetic yang love juice coursing through my veins on doctrines that can directly impact our child.

For example, there is no way in any reality that I will have my son being taught that his heart is "the most deceitful of all things, and desperately wicked." That is just not going to happen. Thankfully, even though my wife is more conservative in her beliefs, we are on the same page there. If we weren't, I would make it known—*respectfully*—nevertheless, passionately. Many people who have grown up with religious parents espousing "worm theology," and within religious communities who have done the same, have horrific opinions of themselves. I should know! I have seen many of them in my therapy office. You can be sure I will never, ever tell my young son that he has a wicked, sick, and evil heart. He has a good heart, partly because he is my son, but mostly because he carries within him the image of God and the Spirit of love. No matter what he does, *that* is his core identity. And I will remind him of that many times throughout his lifetime.

Concluding Remarks

Since this is not a book, but a chapter, I must bid you farewell and leave you with parting words. Being in an Intrafaith relationship can be very challenging. However, it is not impossible. Love, grace, and respect for the dignity of our diverse and complex partners can be our guide. And what a model that can set forth for our children! A monochrome marriage where we give the appearance that there is one truth, and where we believe exactly like each other can set our children up for failure as they depart the family home to enter a multicolored world. When we model emotional regulation, respectful communication, and a firm, loving commitment toward each other while having diametrically opposed ideas–*that* sets them up for success as they journey through life. When they meet classmates with a different religion, race, sexual orientation, or political orientation, they will be well-prepared to prioritize love amidst diversity. That said, may you continue to love well on this wild journey of spiritual metamorphosis.

For those who follow the guide of love and come to a point where that love strangely leads you toward separation or divorce, I leave you with hope, non-judgment, and a blessing. An Intrafaith marriage, where both partners are not on the same page (or even in the same book for that matter), is extremely difficult. Sometimes love is not enough. Sometimes two people can work intensely on a marriage and divorce becomes the sanest (and sometimes the safest) of options, especially for the children's sake. Yet, divorce is not the end. Each new moment and day bring forth rich possibilities for a rewarding and love-saturated future.

I have counseled many couples who did not make it and were in my office at a later point in time with their new fiancé...beaming with pride, happiness, and hopeful expectations. Divorce does not need to be the hopeless end of happiness. It *can* be a new beginning. Above all, wherever you go, whatever you do, let love be your Friend and guide!

11

MAKING SPACE FOR LOVE

By Jon Turney

WHAT HAS THE WORLD come to? That is probably the question most people close to me would ask if they heard that I was writing anything on the subject of parenting. Then, add to that the overlying subject of deconstruction. Now I am sure that they would most definitely think the end of the world is nigh. What are my qualifications, you might ask? What gives me the right to put words to screen to address this topic? Very little, actually.

I do not have a degree in childhood development. I have not studied under any great psychologist. I have not gone to seminary. I do not have a degree in biblical studies. So, where do I get off writing about parenting while deconstructing? Basically, because I have done it. I am doing it. It is the proverbial—*been there, done that*—thing. So, where should we begin? How should I attempt to put down in words what I barely understand myself? I guess like any good story, we should start at the beginning.

To understand who I am you need to have a glimpse into where I came from. I was born in 1970. It was the height of the "Jesus movement." There was a large contingent of "hippies" that had found Jesus and were going back to church in droves. My brother and I were born quite literally in the middle of all of this. My parents weren't hippies but held some similar beliefs with some of these new Christian converts. They grabbed on to the more freeing aspects that this movement offered. My father was "saved" in 1975. I was five at the time, and quite frankly do not have a lot of memories of a time where my dad was not a Christian.

My parents were part of a bible study group that if one was to look at from the outside, one would think that they had just arrived from Haight Ashbury. They had the long hair, the wild clothes, and there was an air about them that was freeing. No more staunch attitudes about faith, religion, or the roles of men and women in the church. At least that is how it looked from the outside. Just like any movement, at some point rules and regulations are put in place to help maintain order. For some reason, there seems to be a need to qualify the roles of both men and women within the church structure.

As the Jesus movement gathered speed, there was this need to address the gender roles both in the church and the home. There was this fear that we could not let the pendulum swing too far from what the church saw as "traditional" roles for both men and women. As my brother and I entered our preteen years this fun-loving group of hippy churchgoers became the "upstanding" adults of the community. They traded in their VW busses for Volvo's. They left behind the bell-bottoms and crazy shirts for suits and nice dresses. They abandoned the notion of fewer rules and regulations for standards, ethics, and morality-based instructions for their children. Gone were the ideas that we could teach our children through love and understanding, and along came the rules and regulations. This was not like turning on a light switch. It was not one way yesterday, and another way today. It was gradual. It was subtle. It went rather unnoticed by most of us children.

I know that I am painting a picture that looks like we were part of a cult. We were not. That being said, I now look at most church environments as some sort of cult. Look at the definition of a cult, and compare it to most churches, and you will see a stark similarity. But I digress. I am not writing about cults...or am I?

My parents were raised by very different people. My mom's mother was a strict woman with strong ideas of the role of women in the home. She was not weak and took care of herself. At the same time, she lived in a world that expected her to keep a nice home, make sure there was dinner on the table, and while doing all this to always look and act respectfully. My dad's mother was also strong and could also take care of herself. She was raised to hold the idea of family as the highest standard. In her world, blood always won out. You took care of yourself and yours before you looked to help anyone else. There is a story in this as well, but again, this is not what I am writing about. But I feel that a little background is important to help you understand who I am and where I came from.

My parents are first and foremost a product of this upbringing. My mom did and does hold herself to this standard. She worked at creating a stable and warm home for us. As much as she could, she kept a clean house and made sure we ate at least a few meals a week as a family. My dad filled the role of the breadwinner in the family. He had a steady job but also filled in the financial gaps with side jobs. I have very fond memories of helping my dad trim trees on the weekend. My work ethic was built around following both of my grandfathers' and my dad's examples. All this being said, there was still a lot of freedom for my siblings and me to be freethinkers and be ourselves.

As finances became scarce our family fell away from the "traditional" roles of family. My mother went to work, which left us kids to fend for ourselves to a certain extent. We got ourselves home after school, and there were days where we left to our own devices for quite a while. The term "latchkey kid" was made popular during this time. I am not sure if I would classify us like that, but we were most definitely "latchkey kid adjacent." This was not all bad either. I can directly connect my love of cooking to these days of having to find and cook meals for myself. During this time, we would go to my mother's parents during summer vacation. It was kept silent, but I know there was a level of dissatisfaction that my mother was a "working" mother. I know that this was a point of contention for my mother. She, on one hand, felt guilty for not always being around when we got home from school, but she also felt a source of pride that she was helping to take care of the family financially. For my father, this was also a double-edged sword. I am sure that he felt both guilt and pride at the same time. Guilt that my mother had to work, and pride that she was doing something that she loved. I stated earlier that I got my work ethic from both of my grandfathers and my father. That is true, but I also acknowledge that my mother was an excellent example of a work ethic for me.

As our family dynamic was changing with my mother going to work, and my brother and I feeling a bit of the freedom that came along with that, the church we were going to was slowly moving away from the freedom of the post "Jesus movement" and starting to become more restrictive and morality based. This was at the beginning of the purity culture that has been such a hot topic lately. We didn't have the purity ring or the purity promises that are so prevalent in that culture. But we were most certainly talked to about the sin of premarital sex and saving ourselves for marriage. There was also a definite dividing line between the way boys and girls were talked to. We heard the basic ideas that we now see as slut-shaming for girls and the notion that "boys will be boys." This put the entire onus on the girls to stay pure and to not tempt the boys into acting out on their unholy nature. Girls were being taught that their role within the family dynamic was important and necessary to help raise the next generation of god-fearing boys and girls. It was time to get back to traditional values where the man provided for the family and the woman was the caretaker of the home and the children.

Some of these teachings were subtle while others were more in your face. Sunday school was a place to indoctrinate young minds into these paths that we were told were biblical and important to correct the path of a lost nation. One that used to be centered around faith, god, and the bible. It was time to course-correct and get back to these values. Little did we know that these teaching would come at the cost of building up walls of shame and fear. We were on a trajectory that took us down the road that taught us that we could not trust our feeling, we could not trust our own hearts, and mostly that the devil was alive and well and leading us and our fellow teenagers astray.

My constant need to ask honest questions, and the church's unwillingness to answer them slowly started to erode my feeling of belonging in the church. During my high school years, I began living a double life. I went to church religiously. I was there Sunday morning, Sunday night, Wednesday youth group, and Saturday night service. I started working when I was 13. I got my first "real" job when I was 15. Having a steady income along with hanging out with people outside of church introduced me to a whole different world. By my senior year of high school, I had all but walked away from the church (in my mind).

My senior year brought another level of disconnect. I am a bass player. I have played bass since the 7th grade. By my senior year of high school, I was rather good at it. My music teacher asked if I would be interested in working on a musical at a local theater. Having never done any type of theater, I was nervous but agreed to give it a go. To say that I was ill prepared for the world of theater would be an understatement. I walked in as a naive, shy, and very quiet teenager. That first show I worked on; I am not sure if I talked to anyone unless I was directly asked a question. What I found fascinating though was this overall arcing love for self and one another. Sure, there was bickering and backbiting. But underlying it all was a mutual respect for the craft. I had never been involved with people that were so open and honest about themselves. Before working in the theater, I was indifferent to the LGBTQIA+ community. They didn't affect me, and I didn't affect them. It was in the theater that I came to a better understanding of the difficulties and hurdles that the LGBTQIA+ community had to deal with on a daily basis. It is where I came to realize that not only were they not "abominations," they were also not any different from me. They just wanted acceptance, respect, and love. They weren't asking for special treatment (which is what I heard time and time again from the church); they just wanted equal treatment. This 18-year-old's worldview was shifting. But at my core was still a high level of shame. The shame of failing god repeatedly. The shame of failing my parents over and over again. This came to a head in two significant ways. I will try to paint a picture of both. These two scenarios sent me on a trajectory that changed the way I viewed god, the church, and how I fit into all of it.

Whether it was due to shyness, anxiety, or the fear of sounding stupid with my myriad questions, I skated by with mostly C's in grades eight through ten. The start of my junior year brought new difficulties, mostly brought on by me. I got my driver's license as soon as I was legally able to. That and a car afforded me the opportunity to go where I wanted when I wanted. I have had some sort of a paying job since I was thirteen and this allowed me to venture farther than some of my schoolmates that did not have a steady income flowing. A mixture of doubting my faith, the intake of some drugs and alcohol, and my need for alone time led me to escape the confines of school quite often.

At first, I was nervous that the school would reach out to my parents to inform them of my lack of attendance at school. It became clear to me rather quickly that for some reason the school either did not know or did not care that I was missing a large portion of my weekly classes. This all culminated in my school grades plummeting. By the end of my junior year, I was getting either D's or F's in all of my classes except for music. I had to go to adult education summer school between my junior and senior years to correct most of the classes I had failed.

Even with summer school, I ended up taking a full load of classes my senior year of high school. While many of my classmates had the opportunity to have half days during their senior year, I was taking a zero period to fit in all the classes I would need to graduate. To say that I was done with school would be an understatement. As the second semester of my senior year started, I officially quit. I did not tell anyone. Not my parents. Not my teachers. I got up every morning as if I was going to school. I would spend seven hours or so driving around and finding other things to do. We had an arcade in town. There were many hours spent in front of video games getting better at one of the only things I felt that I excelled at. I made it sixteen days straight doing this until the school finally reached out to my parents to inform them that I had been missing from all of my classes. I try to imagine the phone call that ensued between the school office and my parents.

School: *Is this Mrs. Turney?*

Mom: *Yes.*

School: *Good. We are calling to inform you that your child has missed the last 16 days of school. We feel that it is important that you know if he fails to show up to another day of classes, he will fail the semester, and because of that, he will not be able to graduate with his class.*

Mom: *Are you sure? Why is this the first I am hearing of this? Why did you not call us sooner? It seems like there should be something in place to ensure this doesn't happen.*

School: *We assure you there is. There seems to have been an oversight when it comes to your son's truancy. We apologize. But that does not diminish the importance that your son needs to not miss any more classes.*

Mom: *Um, OK. His father and I will have to have a conversation with him about it.*

Both parties hang up.

My mother did have the conversation with me. It did not go well if my memory serves me correctly. This next part of my story is painful, and I relive it almost daily. My mother is one of the most loving people I know. She does not ever deserve the anger that someone like me oftentimes directed at her. In a fit of anger and shame, as my mother was trying to talk to me calmly and rationally, I lost my ever-loving mind. I stood up approached my mother. Towering over her, I raised my hand as if to hit her.

In my seventeen years of life, I had never reacted to either of my parents in this manner. Looking back, it still crushes me. I quickly went from complete and utter anger to shame and fear. I saw the look in my mother's eyes as she waited for the coming blow from my hand. The shame took over, and I quickly turned away. I did not hit my mother. But at that moment, I realized there was something immensely wrong with me. I turned and literally ran out the front door. I was leaving. I was never coming back.

How could I ever face my parents again? How could I show my face around any of my family? My family had loved me through everything. This family that might show me anger from time to time, but also grace and forgiveness. In my mind, I had burned the final bridge. I had cast the last lot of my life. I would need to save that money I was spending on video games, alcohol, and drugs. I would have to find a place to live. These are the things that scattered through my mind as I wandered the streets of our town. Mostly I could not bear the looks of my parents when I walked back into the house.

Eventually, I had to wander back. I expected to see my belongings in the front yard, and my dad waiting to have one of his talks with me. As I approached the house, there was no sign of my eviction. My father's car was in the driveway, so I knew he was home. It was time to get this over. It was time to be disowned by my parents and for me to start my new life on my own. I wish I had a better memory of what happened next. But I was numb. I had built walls around myself to protect what was coming next. What I can tell you is that the ultimate showdown did not happen.

My parents, in all their faults and misgiving about their eldest child's problems, came at this situation from a place of love and grace. They went as far as to offer an opportunity to go back to adult education where I had succeeded. Let's make one thing perfectly clear. I was in trouble. Deep trouble. My parents infused themselves into the last semester of my high school career in an almost stifling way. I hated every minute of it. I was doing better, but I was still self-medicating away my anxiety and shame. Because of their diligence, I did graduate with my class with a solid 2.3 GPA. Nothing to brag about, but at least I finished. That is where I thought my story would end as it pertained to education. I figured I would never enter any form of academic life again. I would enter the workforce and that would be that. But along comes circumstance. Along comes opportunity. Along comes someone who saw more in me than I saw in myself. Along came love, but more on that later.

Then came the proverbial final straw. Let me set the scene.

It is Sunday afternoon. Church has just ended. People are moving from people pod to people pod. There is a level of excitement in the air. The pastor had delivered one hell of a sermon today. As I move from group to group, I pick up on each group's conversations. I do not linger long. Most of these people I just know in passing. I finally locate my group. It is made up of people mainly in their late teens. I am eighteen and am getting ready to embark on my post-high school life. I have lingered in the church's youth group mainly because I am afraid of jumping into a college group. Am I ready to grow up? Am I ready for that responsibility? As I approach the group their conversation seems to taper off some as they look at me. Eighteen-year-old me misses the uncomfortable stares and strikes up a conversation with a couple of the group. As we are chatting the youth pastor approaches and asks the group if they would like to come over to their house for a barbecue. We all enthusiastically agree. The group quickly separates and heads toward their individual modes of transportation. We are all still at that age where we want to be the ones driving. Looking back, I am sure this was probably somewhat of a headache for our youth pastors' neighbors having a group of teenagers showing up in all manners of cars, taking up all the parking places. We did not understand carpooling.

As I arrive and look around, I notice that there was not the usual barrage of cars. Thinking I had beat most everyone, I go inside the house. I am taken aback as I walk in and realize that everyone but me is already there. I guess someone got the memo about carpooling. I ask the youth pastor when we are going to barbecue. I am met by a quick glance at everyone in the room and then the response of, "We need to talk first."

I was absolutely living a double life at this time. I pretended to be a good church boy at church on Sunday mornings, Sunday evenings, and Wednesday youth groups. I played their game and pretended that was who I was. At the same time, I was heading down a path that some might call destructive. I was using drugs and alcohol to cover multiple misgivings about religion, faith, and where I belonged in all of it. I had become quite good at hiding it, or so I thought.

I suspect that you are now thinking this is where I admit the error of my ways and show that I repented because of the love of my fellow youth group members. I am sad to inform you that this is not where this story is going. As much as we all want our stories to follow those unrealistic after-school specials. I am here to tell you that they usually do not.

Even though I did not have a word for it at the time, what was about to go down was an intervention. It was an intervention for me, yours truly, the man I see in the mirror. I was asked to not speak but to listen as person after person told me in no uncertain terms the road I was heading down. I heard everything from "You are going to die from a drug overdose" to "Do you want to burn forever in a lake of fire?" I sat there stunned. I would not have been able to speak, even if I had been allowed to. These were my friends. These are the very same people that had sat with me through heartache after heartache. In turn, I had sat with them through their trying times and through their slipping away from the faith. It had never occurred to me to ever come at them like this. To say that I was angry was an understatement.

What they had failed to realize was just how close I already was to leaving the faith altogether. My other life was not because I enjoyed getting drunk and high. It was because those were the few moments when I did not hate myself. Those were the moments when I could hide from my fears. Fears of being a failure, of not living up to what god expected from me, and fear that like every other time, I would inevitably fail at this religious thing again. The other thing that they all failed to understand is that by now I had become an exceptionally good actor. I was living this double life, remember? I knew what they were after. I knew what they needed from me. So, without skipping a beat, I gave them exactly what they expected.

I broke down. I sobbed. I begged for their forgiveness. I cried out to the god that I no longer believed in and pleaded for his forgiveness. The youth pastor escorted me into the kitchen to give me some semblance of privacy as I fell apart. He prayed with me. He hugged me and told me how proud he was of me. What he did not realize is at that moment, religion died in me. I no longer cared what this faith had for me; I did not want any part of it. I hated them all. I hated the youth pastor. I hated the youth group. I hated the church congregation. Most of all I hated their god. What a cruel vindictive bastard he was. I could no longer ignore the obvious disparity between to two gods that were preached on Sundays. The one that loved us no matter what, and the one that would send us to burn for all eternity for some random mistake we intentionally or unintentionally make.

As I was brought back into the living room, my eyes glanced across everyone in the room. I no longer recognized the people in front of me. Those who had always seemed like my friends now had this look of smug satisfaction. I realized that I only mattered as long as these people could save me. I now recognized the same thing in me. How many times had I written someone off as lost? How many times had I given up on someone who had backslidden? Church for these people had become nothing more than a sales transaction. It had become a bean-counting exercise. "How many did you save today?" "How many did we lose today?" Never once was the question, "What can I do to make them feel welcome, right now, just as they are?" Not once did we care beyond the notion of bringing another lost soul to the flock.

Is this story true? Yes. Did it happen to me? Yes. I have kept it vague because I still know some of these people. My goal here is not to call them out. My goal here is to call out a failing of the church. We (I am calling myself out too) need to be willing to sit with these people who are hurting and feel abandoned. I am sure there are people out there who have victory stories involving an intervention. I am positive though, that the failures outweigh the victories.

We need to move past the quick-fix idea and learn to be present in all the moments.

This is not the church. I for one do not believe this is what the church is called to do. The church is not a judicial court. It is not here to lay down the law. It is not here to pass judgment. The church needs to work like a MASH unit. It must be willing to be mobile. It must be willing to care for the wounded and sick. Not just from what we deem as our side, but for all. We need to be there to respect, care, and most of all, love everyone.

Why have I told you these two stories? Why would I add these in a chapter that is supposed to be about parenting while deconstructing? Good question. The answer is that as much as I might not want to admit it, my teenage years formed me. Unfortunately, my faith created a level of shame that I battle with still today. The church created an environment that set me up for failure. Shame is insidious. It repeatedly tells you that there is something very wrong with you. It is something that is so connected to your being that it cannot be overcome.

Looking back, I believe I played the game for a bit longer. In reality, after the intervention, I checked out. It was the beginning of the end for me. It was not much longer than I completely walked away from the church. Keep in mind that this was in 1989-1990. The word deconstruction was not even on the radar. The words that were thrown around were "falling away," "losing your faith," or "walking the slippery slope." Where I now see the word "deconstruction" as somewhat empowering, the words and phrases thrown at me as I left the church compounded the shame that was already prevalent in my life.

As I entered my "adult" years, I met and fell in love with the woman that would become my wife. Our backgrounds and our faith traditions were very different. This presented a problem for quite a few of my family and friends. When they found out that my girlfriend was an atheist, they began to distance themselves from us. As our relationship progressed, it was a constant threat to my religious friends and family. It went as far as some of my "best" friends refusing to be a part of our wedding. I was forced to quickly change my side of the wedding party as a close friend backed out because my fiancé was an atheist. To say that my wife and I had challenges in our relationship would be an understatement. As I said, we come from completely different faith backgrounds.

Even though I had walked away from the church, a lot of the "family" lessons were still central to the way I thought. I had a lot of preconceived notions of the roles of both men and women with the family dynamic. I made some assumptions about how our marriage would go. I figured I would continue to work, and my wife would stay at home. I assumed that we would start having a family, and that was that. My wife had her own ideas as to how this would work. She was already going to college and had no plans of stopping that. She held a full-time job while attending Humboldt State University full-time. I had left school behind after graduating high school. I did not see myself ever entering back into any form of education. I worked for Montgomery Ward (a now-defunct department store) and was on a management track. I was being groomed to have my own store at some point as long as I was willing to move. With the encouragement of my wife, I decided to go to college. I felt that if I was really going to be serious about being a manager in the retail industry, I should take some business classes.

While my wife was attending HSU, I was attending the local community college. There was a little while that we were both going to College of the Redwoods. That was fun. We took a few classes together. My wife is a better student than I am, and it was fun learning how to be a better student from her. I graduated from CR with an Associate of Arts degree with an emphasis in humanities. While at CR I had changed my direction. I was looking at getting a degree in music. Music has always been a part of my life. After graduating from CR, I also attended HSU. My wife was working on a triple major in marine biology, zoology, and biology with an emphasis in microbiology. She also was minoring in English writing. I entered HSU with the plan of becoming either a performer of music or a music teacher. I quickly decided that I wasn't really suited for either. Even though I loved playing music, I did not have the time or patience to reach the level I would need to be to perform at a professional level. I change my major to computer information systems.

My wife and I were both 21 when we got married. Because of some baggage in both of our lives, we made a subconscious decision to not have kids. Looking back, I realize that I was pressuring my wife toward a life-altering decision that she was not ready for. My religious background would rear its ugly head from time to time in the form of questioning my wife as to why she did not want to have kids. Also looking back, I now see that I was nowhere ready to be a parent. In a lot of ways, I was still very much a child myself. I wanted to do the things I wanted when I wanted. I was argumentative. I had a lot of programming that needed to be broken down if I was going to be a good partner in parenting with my wife.

Even though this decision to not have kids right away was not spoken out loud much, it was the best decision for both of us. My wife and I could focus on our college careers. It also allowed us to travel whenever we wanted to do so. We made impromptu trips to quite a few places. If we had started a family right away, these trips would have been fewer, more expensive, and all-around more difficult. Those years were also a time for me to do some growing up (I am still working on this by the way). The walls keeping my preconceived ideas of gender roles were starting to break down. Unfortunately, my walls of shame were not. This will rear its ugly head again and again as my life moves forward.

By 1994, I had changed jobs and was now working for a member-based warehouse club. I was starting all over from the bottom. I did see a bright future with this company and started looking at dropping out of college. I had changed my major three times and was working on being a four-year senior. I began to feel like I was throwing away good money. Shame once again showed up and convinced me to stay in college. I did not want people to see me as a failure. I did not want people to be able to say that I could not follow through on something. I would take semesters off, try to regroup, and then recommit to my studies. Sound familiar?

I did the same thing with religion. I would try really hard, fall away from the faith, then double down and try to be a better Christian. I am sure a therapist would have a heyday looking into that connection. The years went by, my wife and I kept going to college and working our jobs. By then, wife was working at a local veterinarian office and was considering going to school to become one. That would mean moving out of the area. This was fine with me. My job would allow me to transfer to the city we were looking at. Working full-time and going to college full-time takes a toll. It slows down the process and makes it feel like you are getting nowhere. My wife handled this better than I did. I was getting more discouraged with college, while at the same time getting better and better paid at my job. Things all came to a head during my wife's final semester at HSU.

We had been married for eight years at this time. We were both 29 years old. The subject of having kids was coming up more frequently at that time. Honestly, I was the pushy one. I was asking when we thought we should start having kids. At the start of my wife's final semester at HSU, she informed me that she was pregnant. She had taken a home pregnancy test, and it was positive. We went to the local Planned Parenthood to get a more "trustworthy" test, and it also came back positive. Now we had some tough decisions. My wife wanted to finish college, and I wanted her to as well. I decided to drop out. I was floundering and was honestly nowhere near getting a degree. I was just spending money we did not have. My wife made the decision to drop two of her classes. This would change her triple major to a double major. Sadly, she had to drop her favorite major, marine biology. I started going after every management position that came up at work and started working my way up the ladder at work. This enabled my wife to back away from work and only work part-time. We both agreed that we wanted to stay home with our children as much as possible and not put them in daycare if we could afford to make that happen. Neither of us has anything against daycare facilities; we just wanted to be able to be with our child as much as possible.

My wife graduated from Humboldt State University with a double major in Biology and Zoology with a minor in English writing. She was approximately seven months pregnant at the time. Our first child, a daughter, was born that August. To say that this changed everything would be an understatement. Our days of going wherever we wanted, whenever we wanted were over. My wife figured this out way faster than I did. I would ask her out of the blue if she wanted to go see a movie (like we always had done). She would look at me and ask what are we doing with Jo? She's too little to sit through a movie. Looking back, it is funny. I was the one pushing to have kids, and I was the one less prepared for all the changes.

My wife was able to stay at home with our daughter. She still worked part-time but was able to kind of set her own schedule. We were able to set up a schedule that allowed one of us to be home with our daughter most of the time. We relied on family to fill in the few days that our schedules did not mesh. At this point, faith was not a part of the way we raised our daughter. As mentioned earlier, my wife is an atheist, and I had left Christianity behind. Still, there were remnants of the faith that would pop up from time to time. Even as I found pride in my wife's accomplishments in school, I also felt a source of pride that my wife was staying home with our daughter. Unfortunately, I fell into what was a traditional role as the husband/father as well. This became a source of tension between my wife and me as I began to expect a certain lifestyle that came along with these roles.

I did not see the need for me to do any housework. After all, I was at work all day. I was tired when I came home. Was it too much to ask that the house was clean, and there was food ready to eat? I would like to say that this was quickly resolved as I saw the error of my ways. Unfortunately, this was an underlying issue between my wife and me for quite a few years. It was perpetrated by the addition of our oldest son Perrin, in 2002 and our youngest son Korbyn in 2004. These additions just solidified my idea that my wife should stay home with the kids while I worked and brought in the money for us. I was making a good living, we had bought a house, and there was no reason for her to work.

Looking back, I can see how stifling this was. I can see how this was me using a male domineering mindset to control both my wife and kids. This was also anchored in shame. God forbid that we fail at this parenting thing. We had even more to prove than our religious counterparts. We had to show that we could do these parenting things just as well as they could even without god at the center of our parenting. Add to this a ton of medical issues and surgeries with our oldest son, which brought about a whole other level of shame. My faith background told me that our sins would be a course that could follow us and then to our children. Although I did not believe in this faith anymore, it did come to mind as we sat in the recovery room with our son. Sitting in that ICU, I had to ask if I had made some horrible mistakes when it pertained to god. Were we being punished for me not keeping a godly home? I still held onto a Christian type of karma. I still thought that the good you did rewarded you with good, and vice versa. As we sat in the hospital over the years for different surgeries, I would start to calculate all the good I had done in hopes that it would outweigh the potential bad outcome of surgery (this whole story could be at least a chapter on its own).

As my kids got older and entered school, it cleared up some time for my wife. I was still stuck in this mindset that to look like a good family, we had to have a working dad and a stay-at-home mom. Oh sure, I paid lip service to women's rights. I stood in solidarity with them as long as our family was set in a way that looked good to the people around us. This slowly spilled over on my kids. There was an expectation from me as to how my children acted when they were away from us. Nothing gave me more pride than to hear how well behaved our children were. At the core of all of this was shame.

I find it funny how easily shame weasels its way into all facets of our lives. I once again had to prove that we could do this just as well as the religious people. As my children became old enough to ask questions about god and faith, I would hammer home the notion that god was never the answer. God, Christianity, and church were all crutches that people used to answer the unanswerable questions. We did not need any of it. We were working just fine without any of that in our lives (for the most part I still believe this). Let us jump forward again to the summer of 2016.

As we were preparing for my daughter's first year in high school, we were trying to figure out the best way to get her to school every morning. My wife was working at the local community school that our other kids attended. High school was a good 40-minute drive from our home. I worked early mornings and would not be able to get her there. My wife had to be at work early as well. A freak accident at home caused me to be laid up for the whole summer with a spiral fracture to my right leg. I would be out of work for at least 6 months.

As the first day of school approached, it looked as though I would be available to take her. My leg was still a long way from healed, but I was able to drive. This turned into a most amazing time for me. I was able to have a deep and meaningful conversation with my daughter. I was able to see a little into the mind of a young teenage girl. I wish I had the ears to hear it all. But alas, we do the best at the moment. We talked, we laughed, we argued, and we learned. As the first three months of school came up, and I was able to go back to work, we came up with alternative transportation for my daughter. The good part is I was able to still take her to school on Mondays and pick her up every day after work.

Let's go back to the beginning of the school year. I had a routine. I would drop my daughter off at school. I would head to town and go to the mall and walk. My surgeon told me that I should try to walk every day as part of my therapy. After I did that for a while, I would meet my parents for breakfast. This is where faith found its way back in. My dad relentlessly tried to get me to read books by people like Oswald Chambers, G. K. Chesterton, A. W. Tozer, and C. S. Lewis. I finally relented and read a book by C. S. Lewis. I chose him because I at least knew who he was. I had read *The Chronicles of*

Narnia as a child. This time I read *Mere Christianity*. It was life changing. It was a transformative moment for me.

Looking back, I think we all go through this phase where apologists answer a lot of doubts for us connected to our faith. Where I differ is that we make a conscious choice to not camp there. We are searchers. We are questioners. My wife has pointed out that I tend to go in 100% when I think I am on the right trajectory. I do this to the detriment of the people around me. This is exactly what I did when it came to my newfound connection to faith. It consumed me. It was the driving force to every part of my life. I studied and studied and studied. I started reading one author after another, looking for a better and deeper understanding of this new god I had found. Even though I was following a god that to me seemed to be all-inclusive, I was leaving my family behind. I was treading in waters that they were not willing to follow.

As I was being attacked by my fellow "religious" people for my stands on things like women's rights, Black Lives Matter, LGBTQIA+ rights, and Indigenous people's rights, I was leaving my core family behind. Where I thought I was carving a path for them to follow, I was instead putting up roadblocks they could not navigate. Where I saw myself as a new form of "Christ-follower," they saw the same old same old that the world dumps out time and time again. I went from devoutly anti-faith in all ways to pro-faith...as long as it fit the mold I had created. I was becoming just another loud voice in the crowd expounding my truths. Tack onto this a shame that I have never dealt with. It's a shame that tells me that at my core I am a lousy no-good sinner. I am sure you can see the path I was heading down.

I preached tolerance to the world around me and created a stifling world for my wife and my children. I expected them to toe the line and look like good people. I could not let anyone see that we did not have it all together. I had become exactly what I had told them all religious people were. I became a hypocrite. I showed one side of me to everyone else and another side to my family. Where I thought I had found my calling, all I had found was another way to distance myself from my wife and children. I would like to say I figure this out fast, but that would be a bald-faced lie.

I pushed my new ideas on my family for the next seven years. I created a scenario where my wife and kids wanted very little to do with me. Sure, I was pouring out a faith that was inclusive, wrapped up in god's grace, and showered in the love of god for all. At home, I expected my wife and kids to just accept me where I was, but at the same time, I would call them out on what I saw as their problems. This all came to a head during my daughter's senior year of high school. Without getting into all of it, let us just say that my daughter and I were not seeing eye to eye on much of anything.

By that time, I was working nights at my job and was driving both her and my oldest son to school every day. My daughter and I fought almost every day on the way to dropping them off at school. I was unwilling to listen to her side, and she was tired of me being a hypocrite. I was one person to the people in my faith community, and another person at home. I was falling back into the traps of religion. I had a light bulb moment as my daughter turned 18.

She had graduated from high school. She was looking at moving out with her boyfriend. I was at a crossroads. I could continue to follow this idea of faith and potentially lose my family or reevaluate my whole faith again. To basically deconstruct what I had already deconstructed. So, as I was living this life, preaching in a local church, helping run a men's group, leading worship, and posting like crazy all over social media, I found myself deconstructing all over again. I tore it all down. I left no stone unturned. I literally burned it all to the ground again. What was I left with? What remained? It was one word. Family.

I had to first be there for my family. I chose to have this family. I chose to enter into a marriage with a person that I knew was in a completely different place than me when it came to religion. In all our years together, I never gave her the room to be her own person. I expected her to either follow me or at least stay quiet. The same can be said for how I was a father. I did not expect my kids to follow me in my faith journey, but I did expect them to respect me or also stay quiet. I stifled their journey. I ignored the moments where they were trying to come into their own.

As my daughter turned 18, I knew I had some tough decisions ahead of me. Was I going to continue to be the tyrant dad? Or was I willing to be a dad that listens? Was I willing to be a dad that cares about what is really going on in my children's lives? The same can be said about my marriage. Was I going to be someone that stayed in the rut of a marriage that had no give and takes? That had no room for disagreement. I have spent too many years in fear and shame. The last thing I want to do is create an environment where my spouse and children are also held under that yoke. If I am truly going to be a follower of Christ, it starts with this message, "My yoke is easy, and my burden is light." I am absolutely called to offer the same to my kids and to my spouse.

Oh, how I wished I had learned this years ago. Oh, how I wish I did not make a hard burden for my spouse and children. We cannot change the past. But we can course correct. We are offered the opportunity to start over. Are we willing to give the same to our spouses and children? In all actuality, it is not ours to give. But what a wonderful relationship we could have if we just simply made space for differences. If we made space for questions. If we made space for love.

12

SPARE THE COMPASSION, HARM THE CHILD

BY MATTHEW J. DISTEFANO

Those who spare the rod hate their children, but those who love them are diligent to discipline them. — Proverbs 13:24

Marriage is not absolutely for making children. But it is absolutely for making children followers of Jesus.[1] — John Piper

It's extremely important that parents use proper technique if they are going to spank their children. Give your child a warning before each spankable offense. If he deliberately disobeys, inform him of the upcoming spanking, escort him to the designated room, and mete out the punishment. Typically this would involve one or two swats on the buttocks (note that while there may be a transient redness immediately following a spanking, it should never be done in such a way as to bruise a child. Follow up the spanking with a brief review of the offense.[2] — Focus on the Family

BEFORE I GET INTO the meat of this essay, I'll give you a moment to compose yourself after reading that dreadful quote from Focus on the Family. Clean up the vomit you just spewed out. Get a drink of water. Listen to a five-minute meditation video on YouTube. Yell your favorite cuss word into a pillow. And then come back to this book.

Okay, better? Great. Now let's get into it.

If you weren't aware, I live on the fringes of Christianity. At best. It's more likely that I'm just outside the fringes, but I'll let the detractors quibble over the details. Either way, because of my less-than-Christian status, I'm often asked questions like, "What do you do about how to raise your daughter? How do you discipline her?" or "If you don't go to church, what do you tell her about God?" Well, to be honest, not much. God is first and foremost an experience, and my words, jumbled as they often are, would probably only get in the way. Plus, it's my goal to have my daughter unlearn as little as possible, and at this moment in time, it's best to simply model what I think God is like rather than blab on about it.

However, there are some things I teach her, and some things she simply knows from experience, and we are going to cover all of it in the sections that follow. First, though, I want to discuss what I believe are the two biggest problems with how Christian children are often raised—you know, in order to sweep away some of the toxicity before getting to the good stuff.

All Are Welcome?

First, have you ever seen those churches that advertise that all are welcome? Then you check out their statement of faith or listen to just one sermon and realize that you have a different working definition of "welcome?" And "all." And perhaps even "are." Yeah, there are way too many of those places.

These types of Christians—the ones who only pay lip service but don't really mean it—are one reason why my wife and I don't raise our daughter in the church. We don't want her to grow up thinking that it's okay to call exclusion by its opposite name.

Now, that is not to say there aren't truly inclusive churches—churches that really do welcome the LGBTQIA+ members, churches that really are in the business of racial reconciliation, churches that really do lift up and celebrate non-Christians. Unfortunately, these churches are few and far between. More commonplace are the churches who teach children to reject those who are not like them, to reject their non-Christian friends, to approach their peers only with the clandestine agenda to convert them. Think back to the Piper quote I used above. Pay attention to the language he uses: "*Making* children followers of Jesus.*"[3] Making. Forcing. *You will do this*. Not teaching them what Jesus-following looks like. Not letting them choose for themselves. Making them do it.

This runs counter to what children naturally do in life. Without imposing our agendas on them, they view the world with wonder and awe. They include their friends, no matter what their friends look like, which God they worship, whom they love, how much money they have or don't have, and so on. It's only when we force them to do something, do they turn into the exclusionary Christians people so often equate with Christ.

Spare the Rod, Spoil the Child?

The second issue when it comes to child-rearing is that Christianity—the Christianity I myself grew up with—argues in favor of a punitive and physical form of discipline. It was often said how kids will become spoiled brats if they are not spanked. After all, the Bible was clear.

Except it's not. And that's okay. The Bible shouldn't be our authority on this matter anyway. And even if it is our authority, even if the aforementioned quote from Proverbs is to be our measuring stick for what good parenting looks like, it is but an analogy. I mean, are any Christians today arguing in favor of hitting their kids with literal rods? God, I hope not!

As an analogy, though, I'll admit that it can work. Discipline is healthy. As the writer of Hebrews states, "Discipline always seems painful rather than pleasant at the time, but later it yields the peaceful fruit of righteousness to those who have been trained by it."[4] But discipline need not involve spanking. The two are not synonyms.

What Does the Science Say?

Not only can discipline be instilled without including corporal punishment, the science says that physical punishment should never be used. According to the American Academy of Pediatrics, "Aversive disciplinary strategies, including all forms of corporal punishment and yelling at or shaming children, are minimally effective in the short-term and not effective in the long-term. With new evidence, researchers link corporal punishment to an increased risk of negative behavioral, cognitive, psychosocial, and emotional outcomes for children."[5] The American Psychological Association is in agreement. Writing for *The Monitor*, Brendan L. Smith cites various professionals, including University of Michigan's Sandra Graham-Bermann, PhD, Yale's Alan Kazdin, PhD, and University of Connecticut's Preston Britner, PhD, who all agree that physical punishment causes long-lasting harm.[6] Smith concludes: "Many studies have shown that physical punishment—including spanking, hitting and other means of causing pain—can lead to increased aggression, antisocial behavior, physical injury and mental health problems for childre n."[7]

Unfortunately, as Smith would later point out, roughly two-thirds of Americans *still* approve of parents spanking their kids.[8] Why is this the case? I can only guess. To my mind, the reasons are at least two-fold.

Old-Time Religion

The first reason I believe the majority of Americans still support parents hitting—ahem, spanking—their children is because it goes hand in hand with their religion. What I mean is that their theology matches up with physical punishment. Think about it. When you imagine what type of God most people believe in, what image comes to mind? Unless you've deconstructed your old-timey religious views, you probably picture a judge. Perhaps you imagine a big white dude in the sky, meting out punishment on the so-called wicked. I'm guessing you believe there is an eternal hell for those who don't make the cut. I could continue, but you probably get the point: We parent in the same way our God "parents" us.

The reason for this is pretty simple. We are mimetic beings. If you've read my book, *Heretic!*, you know what I mean by that. We imitate those whom we look up to. If our model of desire dresses a certain way, we dress a certain way. If our model of desire has a certain car, we desire a certain car. If our God is a punitive disciplinarian, we tend toward being a punitive disciplinarian. And frankly, the God of many a Christian is just that—perhaps loving when he wants to be but cross him, and you'll get his more wrathful and vengeful side.

Change is Hard

The second issue I see when it comes to our society's insistence on hitting kids is that change is difficult. If you are thirty or forty or older, you probably grew up in a home where spanking was a common practice. That's because our parents, the so-called Baby Boomers, were raised by parents who hit them with all sorts of household items—spatulas, flip-flops, whatever happened to be in their hands at the time. Our parents generally moved away from that a bit and just used their hands or, at worst, a belt. And now, hopefully, we can start moving away from that outdated idea and embrace a more compassionate, science-driven model.

Again though, change is hard and turning a big ship takes time. It takes time to educate people on this issue, so all I can say is that if you are reading this and you agree with me, be that change. Start in your own home and then move outside your borders. The more of us who do that, the quicker that needed change will come.

Compassionate Inclusion, Compassionate Discipline

Okay, so it's obvious that this chapter is not going to argue in favor of either limited inclusion or corporal punishment. That much is clear. But what do we replace these ideas with? What do we replace top-down authoritarianism with? How do we go about teaching our children to include everyone, regardless of race, religion, color, creed, or sexual orientation? Also, how do we discipline our children compassionately, without using physical violence, harsh language, or even threats? Well, that's going to take some creativity and patience, but in the end will hopefully be well worth it.

First off, when it comes to inclusion and whom our children accept, we probably don't have to teach them much. For many, it will be more about unteaching. As I said earlier, children tend to approach the world with awe and wonder. It's only when we impress upon them our messed-up ideas that they turn into little tyrants. If we remove our need to make them think in certain ways, they tend to be much more well-rounded and accepting.

Take, for instance, my daughter Elyse. We've never necessarily *taught* her to affirm the LGBTQIA+ community. She just knew it was right to accept who people are. Full stop. When I came out to her as bisexual, then, her response was, "So?" Not because she doesn't care about me, but because it's such a non-issue that she couldn't understand why I thought it was newsworthy. For me to accept myself, on the other hand—given that I was taught anything other than hetero is sinful—it took much more time and effort. For her, it was a no brainer.

Focusing now on discipline: This is where many need to take a one-eighty and become way more inclusive. What I mean is that when you discipline your children, you include them in the process. It's never a "power over" thing, but a "power with" thing. "Power over" is the old model. That model uses phrases like, "Because I said so." That model is all about telling children what to do because you are their parent, and they should blindly follow your authority. In contrast, when you have a "power with" model, you stand alongside them and help them see for themselves where they are going astray. You ask things like, "What do you think will happen if you continue to do that?" or "If your friends were treating you how you are treating me, how do you think you'd feel?"

Of course, asking rhetorical questions will not be the end-all-be-all solution to your problems as a parent. Your children will push back. They will give you attitude. Not everything will be smooth sailing. However, the more consistent you become, the more your child will work in tandem with you, rather than fighting you at every step along the way. You have to show them how to do this, however. Being an authoritarian will only teach them to eventually be authoritarians themselves. Remember, we are mimetic beings.

The more you implement a "power with" approach, though, the more your relationship with your child will blossom. But you need three components: Respect, collaboration, and limitation.[9]

1. Respect: See your children as individuals, valuing their feelings and views.

2. Collaboration: Work together with your children and adapt to issues that arise.

3. Limitation: Impose age and maturity-appropriate boundaries, keeping in mind their safety and security.

With these three components in place, your role as a parent can move from the need to control the situation into true, authentic relationship with your child. When your child feels respected and valued, they feel heard. When you and your child collaborate, your relationship strengthens as you use your creativity to come up to solutions to complex problems. And when you put in place appropriate boundaries, you are encouraged to explain your reasoning, which creates dialogue, again leading to a stronger relationship.

Is any of this easy? No, not necessarily. In the moment, we may feel like yelling "Because I said!" Perhaps doing so will even "work." Maybe that top-down approach will get your kids to do what you want from time to time. But will that lead to happy, healthy children? The data says "no."

What Compassionate Parenting Looks Like

Some of you may be thinking that this model is "soft," that it will only lead to unruly children. But let's not conflate compassion with passive. This isn't passiveness. In fact, this model requires consistency and diligent activity. Psychologist Johanna Marie Kalkreuth lays out four key steps one must take to instill compassion-forward discipline.[10]

Inner Discipline

Earlier, I mentioned mimesis with regards to imitating the Gods we believe in. But mimesis isn't just about God. In fact, it is first and foremost a human thing. Kids, then, first learn by imitating their parents. To that end, if a parent is self-disciplined herself, there is likely to be an imitative learning that happens for the child. So, instead of "monkey see, monkey do," we have "child see, child do."

Real-World Application: Think of all the conflicts that married couples get into over the course of their marriage. These can all be opportunities to model what it is like to work through an issue together, while maintaining healthy boundaries and respect for one another. Don't hide all your issues behind closed doors. Some problems, if age-appropriate for the child to witness, can be resolved in front of them. Allow them to see that relationships can be messy and yet, still maintain healthy respect.

Relationship

If you truly want your children to succeed in this area, you have to develop a strong relationship. Again, this isn't primarily a "top down" relationship, where you are the ruling king or queen, but one of mutual respect and care. In other words, you don't get your children to do something because they fear you; you get them to do something because you've cultivated a trusting relationship.

Real-World Application: Be an open book with your child. Tell them about what you were like as a kid, and don't be afraid to share some of the juicy details. Put aside your ego and allow yourself to be embarrassed. You child will typically respect you for that. Don't put yourself on a pedestal and think that what you child requires is a pristine parent. They need someone they can trust to be real and vulnerable with them.

Age-Appropriate Goals

You wouldn't expect a tomato sprout to pump out vine-ripe tomatoes, so don't expect your five-year-old to act like a thirty-five-year-old philosopher king. If you have goals for your children that aren't age-appropriate, you are setting them up for failure. Frustration. Insecurity. This will only lead to behavioral issues.

Real-World Application: Keep the lines of communication open. Have your child set goals for themselves, and then chat with them about how they will go about accomplishing them. Don't get into power struggles. If there are needs to be met—bathing, feeding, cleaning, etc.—give them the expectation, but allow them to come up with solutions as to how they will accomplish them. And always adjust as needed. These are goals you put in pencil, not upon a stone tablet.

Growth Opportunities

Children are going to make mistakes. They are going to process things in ways that you as an adult don't quite understand. Allow them to do this in safe, manageable environments. This is part of the relational aspect of compassionate parenting. Don't punish their mistakes. Point them out and encourage them to learn and grow from those mistakes. As the old adage goes, "The only real mistake is the one from which we learn nothing."[11]

Real-World Application: Kids are going to fail at their goals. They are going to forget to clean up after themselves. They are going to forget to finish their homework. They'll fight you about whether they need to take a shower. Let them make a mistake from time to time. Mistakes, in safe and secure environments, are just fine. If they don't finish one math sheet, let them face their teacher the next day. If they don't pick up their room, maybe the puppy happens to chew something of theirs that they like. Natural consequences go a long way, and closely managed mistakes can be great teaching tools.

Now, please don't think of these four key steps in a linear sort of way. They aren't that. You don't go from Step One to Step Two to Step Three to Step Four. These are four areas of growth you and your child are working on at the same time. For example, while you work on your inner discipline (Step One), you are implementing age-appropriate goals (Step Three), which your child will sometimes not achieve, thus leading to their growth (Step Four). All the while, you are observing and taking note, supporting them along the way. This leads to a trusting relationship that strengthens over time (Step Two).

Again, this is by no means a passive system. It requires patience and consistency, but if implemented, gives your child the best opportunity to grow into a happy, healthy individual. As Dr. Kelkreuth so eloquently puts it:

> Compassionate, relationship-based discipline [. . .] allows a child to grow into their next developmental phase in a healthy way, held by strong boundaries, loving connection, and a sense of security. It allows the greatest potential and highest functioning of the child to grow and flourish.[12]

Some Final Thoughts

Let me be clear: none of what I said throughout this essay is meant to shame parents who have taken a more punitive approach. If you have spanked your child or have been less than inclusive in your parenting style, you are not an evil person. My parents' generation didn't have the data we now have. They were all working with what they had. However, now that we have more robust data when it comes to certain parenting practices, we can implement better practices. It doesn't stop with us, though. In the future, our children and children's children will likely have even more data and will hopefully build upon what we now know. The point is that we continue to grow and progress.

So, thinking back to the quote from the book of Proverbs; yes, to love your children is to discipline them. The question, then, is how do we do this? Do we rule our homes with an iron fist, instilling the so-called fear of God in them? Do we come down upon them like a Nero or a Caligula? Hell no! We stand beside them and guide them. We practice inner discipline ourselves, and then model for them what doing right looks like. We replace "power over" with "power with." Because when we do this, we not only help them grow and flourish, but we also strengthen our bond with them. They no longer see us as an authoritarian; they start seeing us as a mentor and a guide. It's a different kind of authority, one that values the autonomy of the child and helps lift them up with dignity and honor.

13

BEFORE WE GO

By Jason Elam

You might remember our oldest daughter, Alex, who I introduced to you in the Introduction of this book. After living in an apartment with roommates for nearly a year, she recently came home for a few days while she was recovering from wisdom tooth surgery. It was healing for us that she chose to come home when she wasn't feeling well. She has a seemingly endless number of friends who all would have been thrilled to be her nurse for a few days, but she wanted to come home.

Our insecurities told us that we had failed as Alex's parents to the point that there could be irreversible damage to the relationship. After all, we made just about every dumb mistake that parents can reasonably make with their kids. But, in the end, once we saw her as a human being to be loved and not controlled, she turned back to us. We're so grateful.

Brandi and I are not parenting experts by any stretch of the imagination, but there are some things that we have learned in the process of compiling and editing this book.

Apologies Let the Healing Waters Flow

Every healing conversation starts with a recognition of what the child is feeling in that moment. Often, an apology from the parent is necessary for the air to be cleared and for the child to let their guard down long enough to let you in. Don't hold back or choose your words too carefully. Own your mistakes. Fall on your sword, if necessary. This is no time for saving face. Your relationship with your child is more important than your pride.

Kids Have the Right to Forge Their Own Path

This one was a real struggle for me. The model that I was raised with stated that parents implement the path and the children learn to follow it as they grow into adulthood. I just don't think that model leaves room for the child to be their authentic self. We aren't trying to raise Stepford Children here. There is no one size fits all method of parenting that will guarantee that our kids grown into perfect and successful grown-ups; whatever that means. The older I get, the more I believe that our kids should take the lead in the direction of their own lives as soon as it's practically safe for them to do so. That doesn't mean they are ready to make life and death decisions whenever they think they are. It just means that, as parents who love them, we are always on the lookout for opportunities to let them grow in their agency and flex their wings.

When it comes to our child's spiritual life, they have full agency. They call the shots. Forcing a child to go to church is a perfect way to make sure that they never go as adults. On the other hand, if your child finds joy and peace in a church setting then let them go without having to overcome a multitude of objections from you. We don't want to be the one to ruin what is otherwise a positive thing in our child's life. As they mature, they may outgrow their need for religion. They may not. The only thing that really matters is that they know you love them and want them to succeed in life.

A Final Thought

Love is the reason we're here. We have come from love, were created in love and by love, and have been imbued with love to make this world a better place.

There's no higher calling than love, especially when it comes to our children.

Loving our kids fully and completely means getting to know who they really are—even the parts they might be tempted to hide from us. Every interaction with our kids helps them know whether it's safe for them to entrust a part of themselves to us or not. When we choose to rigidly enforce rules and punishment, it sends the message that our preconceived notions of our kids should be are more important to us than knowing and understanding who they really are.

Look for opportunities to earn your child's trust and when they reach out to you in trust to reveal some new facet of who they are, lavishly love and celebrate that part of them.

The greatest freedom in life is to be fully known and fully loved. Giving our child a lifetime of that freedom—starting today—is the best gift we can ever give them.

As parents, we're going to make mistakes. I'm sure, like me, you've already made more than you care to count. But if we can love our kids and make sure that they feel how loved and accepted they have always been, then we can help set them for a life of living as their authentic selves.

As parents, what could be better than that?

END NOTES

PREFACE

1. Proverbs 22:6.

2. The Deconstruction Network—Initial Survey, 2020.

3. For an in-depth breakdown of deconstruction see my video series "understanding deconstruction" on YouTube or at:

https://www.thedeconstructionnetwork.com/understanding-deconstruction.

4. Pew Research Center, 2015.

5. General Social Survey, 2018.

6. Public Religious Research Institute, 2020.

7. Packard & Hope, 2014—see also their great book, *Church Refugees*, 2015.

8. General Social Survey, 2018.

9. Lifeway Research, 2019.

10. Public Religious Research Institute, 2016.

11. Pew Research Center, 2020.

12. Developmental Theory is a branch of psychology (bleeding into sociology, anthropology, and even philosophy) that looks at the science of how people develop. The most common field people will know about is Child Development Theory . . . the idea that there are different stages children must go through to develop healthily, developing an ego (the terrible twos) developing empathy (4-6), etc.

INTRODUCTION

1. Proverbs 22:6.

CHAPTER 2

1. Proverbs 13:22.

2. Psalm 23:4.

3. Proverbs 13:24.

CHAPTER 3

1. A group that promoted communication, public speaking, and leadership.

2. Refer to the works of Carl Jung on "shadow."

CHAPTER 5

1. Proverbs 22:6.

2. Bettelheim, B. (1995). *A good enough parent: the guide to bringing up your child.* Thames and Hudson.

3. Phelan, T. W. (2014). *1-2-3 magic.* ParentMagic, Inc.

CHAPTER 9

1. John 1:5.

2. John 1:3.

3. Colossians 1:16.

4. John 14:20.

5. Romans 5:19.

6. 1 Corinthians 15:22.

7. Galatians 2:20.

CHAPTER 10

1. Read more at https://www.gottman.com/blog/softening-startup/.

2. v. 24, emphasis mine.

3. For more self-compassion practices and meditations, you can go here: https://selfcompas sion.org/category/exercises/.

4. Adapted from Russ Harris, *ACT Made Simple: An Easy-to-Read Primer on Acceptance and Com mitment Therapy*. 2nd ed. (Oakland, CA: New Harbinger Publications, Inc., 2019), 229.

CHAPTER 12

1. Piper, John. *This Momentary Marriage: A Parable of Permanence*. Wheaton: Crossway, 2012, 93.

2. From Focus on the Family, "Questions About Spanking," which can be found at http://www.fo cusonthefamily.com/family-qa/questions-about-spanking/.

3. Piper, John. *This Momentary Marriage: A Parable of Permanence*. Wheaton: Crossway, 2012, 93.

4. Hebrews 12:11.

5. Sege, Robert D., and Siegel, Benjamin S. "Effective Discipline to Raise Healthy Children." In *Pediatrics*. Vol. 142, Issue 6. December 1, 2018, Abstract, para 1.

6. Smith, Brian L. "The Case Against Spanking." *American Psychological Association*. Vol. 43. No. 4. April 2021. http://www.apa.org/monitor/2021/04/spanking, en toto.

7. Ibid., para 3.

8. Ibid.

9. Pribanova, Maddie. "Compassionate Discipline." *Center for Educational Improvement*. (September 18, 2018). https://www.edimprovement.org/post/compassionate-discipline.

10. Kalkreuth, Johanna Marie. "Compassionate Discipline: Further Explained." *Institute of Child Psychology*. (October 26, 2020). http://instituteofchildpsychology.com/compassionate-discipline-fu rtherexplained/, en toto.

11. Quote by Henry Ford, unknown source.

12. Kalkreuth, Johanna Marie. "Compassionate Discipline: Further Explained." *Institute of Child Psychology*. (October 26, 2020). http://instituteofchildpsychology.com/compassionate-discipline-furtherexplained/, para 8.

For more information about Jason and Brandi Elam,
or to contact him for speaking engagements,
please visit www.patheos.com/blogs/messyspirituality/.

Many Voices. One Message.

Quoir is a boutique publisher
with a singular message: *Christ is all*.
Venture beyond your boundaries to discover Christ
in ways you never thought possible.

For more information, please visit
www.quoir.com

CPSIA information can be obtained
at www.ICGtesting.com
Printed in the USA
BVHW031818261122
652660BV00007B/539